SPECIAL INTERESTS

HOW LOBBYISTS INFLUENCE
LEGISLATION

Jules Archer
History for Young Readers

SPECIAL INTERESTS

HOW LOBBYISTS INFLUENCE LEGISLATION

JULES ARCHER

Sky Pony Press
NEW YORK

Historical texts often reflect the time period in which they were written, and new information is constantly being discovered. This book was originally published in 1997, and much has changed since then. While every effort has been made to bring this book up to date, it is important to consult multiple sources when doing research.

To Dorothy Soule
For everything

CONTENTS

SPECIAL INTERESTS

LIST OF ABBREVIATIONS

(D-CT)	Democrat from Connecticut (or other state)
(R-FL)	Republican from Florida (or other state)
Rep.	Representative in the House
Sen.	Senator in the Senate
AARP	American Association of Retired People
ADA	Americans for Democratic Action
AIPAC	American Israel Political Action Committee
AMA	American Medical Association
CRP	Committee to Re-elect the President (Nixon)
CUBs	Citizens Utility Boards
EPA	Federal Environment Protection Agency
FDA	Food and Drug Administration
FEC	Federal Election Committee
FTC	Federal Trade Commission
GAO	General Accounting Office
GOP	"Grand Old Party"—the Republican party
HUD	Department of Housing and Urban Development
NAFTA	North American Free Trade Agreement
NAM	National Association of Manufacturers
NEA	National Education Association
NRA	National Rifle Association
NRLC	National Right to Life Committee
PAC	Political Action Committee
SBA	Small Business Association
SEC	Securities and Exchange Commission
S&Ls	Savings and Loan banks
WPA	Works Project Administration

Politicians of both parties outwardly agree that the American lobbying system is in need of reform. But when will they have the courage to do something about it?

I

Who and What Are Lobbyists?

"Public opinion shows that a majority of Americans feel that lobbyists are the real power in Washington," declared Sen. Carl Levin (D-MI) in 1995. "Only 22 percent believes it's the president. We must act to restore confidence that in fact their representatives control the power in Washington."[1]

In our democracy the laws and regulations we live under are made by representatives that we elect to public office and by the government commissions and agencies that they in turn appoint to carry out this legislation. Lobbyists are privately employed agents, working as individuals or in firms, who are allowed to pressure these lawmakers into passing laws and regulations that would benefit their clients.

The original term for lobbyists was "lobby agents," so-called because they petitioned lawmakers in the lobbies, or anterooms, of the legislative chambers. The designation for these individual agents soon became shortened to lobbyists. Groups or organizations that petition are called lobbies. The act of petitioning lawmakers is referred to as lobbying. Because the term "lobbyist" has longstanding dubious implications in the public mind and because a legal requirement to register as a lobbyist imposes certain limitations, some lobbyists prefer to call themselves "legislative consultants."[2]

Lawmakers meet regularly with lobbyists who provide campaign contributions. These meetings give lobbyists the opportunity to provide legislators with information favorable to their clients, which legislators can use when justifying votes for the clients' benefit. It is no secret that many lobbies seeking legislation favoring important special interests exercise great power. Some legislators even allow lobbyists to write the bills that the legislators introduce. This also happens in state, county, and city lawmaking bodies. Jake Arvey, former head of the Cook County, Illinois, Democratic party, once defined politics as "the art of putting people under obligation to you."

Legislators whose votes favor the clients of lobbyists are rewarded with large contributions for their election and reelection campaigns. Getting elected to public office is an expensive process, requiring huge campaign funds. Most of these campaign funds come from special-interest lobbies.

According to the Commerce Department, the 1992 presidential election campaigns, for example, cost $3.2 billion, triple what they had cost a dozen years earlier. Presidential candidates spent about $550 million, and congressional candidates another $678 million. Political parties and political action committees (PACs) spent almost $1 billion on national races. Candidates in state and local elections spent another $1 billion.

"The relationship between large campaign contributions and an individual congressman's support of legislation favored by the contributors," observed the Birmingham, Ala., *Post-Herald,* "has long been plain to anybody who cares to look. . . . It doesn't do much for public confidence in Congress' dedication to the public interest."

In addition to providing campaign funds, lobbyists also repay legislators, commissioners, and their chief aides with special

Cartoonist Tom Gibb puts a new spin on a statement made by Colin Powell as he declined a potential presidential nomination. He cites the three greatest problems in American politics, two of which are a direct result of the lobbying system.

favors, such as free travel, vacations, and entertainment. These officials are invited to speak before business groups for fat fees.

Lobbyists also work through the media. They organize local campaigns to get voters to flood Congress with letters, telegrams, e-mail, and phone calls. They provide and coach witnesses to testify before congressional committees in praise of clients' bills. Lobbyists may solicit movie and sports stars to appear at fund-raisers for political candidates. Fund-raisers are dinners or other events sponsored by lobbyists for candidates to which business executives seeking favorable legislation are invited and expected to contribute campaign funds.[3]

In 1979, *The New York Times* reported that in the previous fall's congressional elections, special interests had contributed almost $1 million to the campaigns of just eight congressional leaders. Few realists expected those congressmen to vote against any bills that those lobbies wanted passed. Some lobbies contribute campaign funds to rival candidates in an election, so that no matter which one wins, the lobbies are guaranteed the ear of the winner.

If the lobbying processes are carried out in the manner originally intended, which is to encourage communication between government officials and private citizens or groups that have grievances or proposals, the result can often be new legislation that is beneficial to the country.

In the July 10, 1996, issue of the *Conservative Chronicle*, Stephen Chapman defends the use of money in lobbying. "Money is an indispensable element of democracy," he declares, "and one that will find a way to infiltrate no matter how many laws are passed to keep it out. The reason is that politics is about communicating ideas, and communicating ideas requires cash."

He cites a report by the Committee for the Study of the American Elections, which states that "the crucial financial determination of election outcome is not how much the top

HOW BILLS BECOME LAWS

How a Bill Is Passed

Because members of Congress and their staffs do not have the time or special knowledge to evaluate every bill introduced into the legislative hopper, bills are first routed to special legislative committees dealing with matters they affect. The committees study these bills, sometimes holding hearings to listen to their advocates and opponents. Some lobbyists are called upon to give testimony at these hearings, providing expertise that helps inform committee members and answering their questions about the need for and effects of proposed legislation. As a result of their testimony, the committee may decide to recommend a bill, reject it, or table it for further consideration.

When a bill is sent to the full House or Senate with a committee recommendation, its passage is often assured. Because of this special power of congressional committees, their chairpersons, staffs, and committee members are prime targets for lobbyists. Those legislators, especially the chairpersons, collect a lion's share of election campaign contributions from big businesses affected by their decisions.

1. Lobbyists often start the ball rolling by proposing a bill to a congressman or senator.
2. The lawmaker introduces the bill in the House or Senate.
3. The bill is sent to the committee responsible for handling such bills; for example, a finance bill would be sent to the finance committee.
4. The committee may recommend, reject, or table the bill.

5. The committee may decide to hold hearings on important bills to let advocates and opponents present their views.
6. Lobbyists or experts for and against the bill may be called upon to testify.
7. If the committee recommends the bill, it is sent to the full House or Senate for a vote.
8. If the bill passes, it is then sent to the opposite chamber—House or Senate—where it is referred to the proper committee, and goes through the same committee process described in steps 4, 5, and 6 above.
9. If there are differences of opinion, House and Senate leaders meet to try to work out a compromise bill.
10. If both houses pass the bill, it goes to the president, who may either sign it into law or veto it.
11. If the president vetoes the bill, the vote of two-thirds of Congress is necessary to pass the bill over the veto.

spender invests in a campaign, but whether other serious candidates have sufficient funds to get their message to the voters."

But the Bill of Rights certainly never intended the redress of grievances to be influenced by whether or not legislators received campaign contributions or gifts from petitioners.

THE ORIGINS OF LOBBYING IN AMERICA

Lobbies are nothing new in the United States. They existed even before we became a nation. In 1757 the Pennsylvania colonial assembly sent Benjamin Franklin to England to lobby Parliament not to pass the Stamp Act, which required colonists to pay a tax for official seals on all newspapers and legal documents.

There is nothing illegal about the act of lobbying. The right of any person or group to "petition the government for a redress of grievances" was and is protected by the First Amendment. Thomas Jefferson insisted upon this amendment, mindful of the refusal of the British government to listen to the grievances of the American colonists, which brought on the American Revolution.

James Madison feared that majority factions in America might force passage of laws that favored them. He saw lobbies as one way to prevent a permanent majority bloc from forming. If Americans were not free either to promote or fight change through lobbies, Madison feared, then a party in power might wield dictatorial control over the country.[4]

Early America was a country of vast distances, with many Americans remote from state and national governments. Travel was lengthy and time-consuming, as well as difficult, so that lobbyists who advanced their grievances to government officials often performed a valuable service. Lobbyists were petitioners with either their own grievances that they sought to set straight, or with the grievances of interests that they represented.

Lawmakers often appreciated the information they received from lobbyists because their own knowledge in many special areas, and the time involved to acquire it, was extremely limited. Even when lobbyists represented private interests for profit, the projects they helped legislate spanned the growing nation with essential roads, canals, bridges, and schools, as well as provided millions of jobs.

As early as 1852, however, congressional lobbies were a cause for concern. James Buchanan wrote to President Franklin Pierce, who had defeated him for the Democratic nomination: "The host of contractors, speculators, stock-jobbers, and lobby members which haunt the halls of Congress, all desirous . . . on any and every pretext to get their arms into the public treasury are sufficient to alarm every friend of his country."[5]

"Father, dear Father, come home!"

The three-way tension between special-interest groups, government officials, and the American public is not new to American politics. This turn-of-the-century cartoon shows the public as a crying child trying to get her daddy (the current attorney general) out of a bar where he is being lavishly plied with liquor by the various lobbies of the day.

Multimillionaire Cornelius Vanderbilt was one of the powerful men in the nineteenth century known as "robber barons." They were extremely wealthy men who made their fortunes by charging exorbitant utility rates and by lobbying successfully for government subsidies. Vanderbilt's lobbyists won subsidies for his steamship companies by inviting lawmakers to gamble at a casino that Vanderbilt controlled. Members of Congress who agreed to vote for his government subsidies were allowed to win big sums; or if they piled up gambling debts, they were offered forgiveness.

In 1873, Wisconsin Chief Justice Edward Ryan warned, "Money as a political influence is essentially corrupt . . . dangerous to the free and just administration of the law."

In 1902 the NAM (National Association of Manufacturers) lobby worked to defeat labor bills calling for an eight-hour day and other benefits for workingmen. Congressmen who refused to oblige the lobby were defeated in the 1904 elections by heavy NAM contributions to their rivals.

At the turn of the century a group of investigative reporters whom President Theodore Roosevelt labeled "muckrakers" (because they raked up political scandal) exposed the connection between corporate lobbies and the politicians they controlled.

"Political corruption," Lincoln Steffens wrote in 1906, "was a regularly established custom of the country, by which our political leaders conduct the government of the city, state and nation, not for the common good, but for the special interests of private business." His investigations in the early twentieth century proved that lobbyists were corrupting many city, state, and federal legislatures.[6]

"GOOD" VS. "BAD" LOBBIES

At a 1948 press conference a reporter asked President Harry Truman, "Mr. President . . . would you be against lobbyists who are working for your program?"

President Theodore Roosevelt is shown investigating the meat-packing scandal, but with little enthusiasm. The investigation was undertaken because of the pressure put on Congress by Lincoln Steffens, one of a group of investigative journalists known as muckrakers. The success of the muckrakers in drawing attention to various social evils is an early example of the positive potential of lobbying.

Truman grinned and replied, "Well, that's a different matter. We probably wouldn't call those people lobbyists. We would call them citizens appearing in the public interest."[7]

We need to be thoughtful about what constitutes the public interest. Our history is replete with lobbies that appealed to Congress on behalf of what was clearly a genuine public interest —the correction of social injustice. Lobbyists before the Civil War sought to compel Congress to outlaw slavery. In the 1890s farmers formed a lobby to pressure Congress for farm-support laws to help poor farmers and stop bank foreclosures. Populist Mary Ellen Lease, known as the "Kansas Pythoness," told farmers to "raise less corn and more hell." She said, "Wall Street owns the country. It is no longer a government of the people, by the people, for the people, but a government of Wall Street, by Wall Street, and for Wall Street. Our laws are the output of a system that clothes rascals in robes and honesty in rags!"

To pressure the Congress of 1894 for legislation aiding those who were made jobless by a business depression that shut down factories, Jacob S. Coxey of Ohio led a march of 500 men— "Coxey's army"—to lobby Washington for relief. The suffragettes lobbied with parades and demonstrations instead of money to give women the vote.

Time magazine reported on June 3, 1996, that Marian Wright Edelman, president of the Children's Defense Fund, has been lobbying for 25 years on behalf of children's rights. "I knew it would take 20 years, 25 years to seed a movement," she explained. "You just have to keep planting and watering and fertilizing. And then, when it is time, you do what you have to do."

She summoned Americans to a rally at the Lincoln Memorial to "Stand for Children." Challenging congressional budget cuts, she declared, "Children are never going to get what they need until there is a change in the ethos that says it is not acceptable to cut children first."

Edelman's persistent lobbying helped produce the result of a *Time* magazine poll that showed 73 percent of Americans want more of their tax dollars going to programs that benefit the young. In the late 1980s the Children's Defense Fund put together a coalition that was instrumental in the 1990 passage of a multibillion-dollar childcare bill for low-income working parents.

Can we make the distinction between good and bad lobbyists? Good and bad are subjective terms and depend upon who is making the judgment. A good lobby, however, may be defined as one that seeks legislation that is clearly in the public interest, such as laws that promote health, education, fair elections, child welfare, and clean air and water. Perhaps the most plausible definition of a bad lobby is one that uses money contributions to bribe legislators or government officials to favor legislation for its clients, or to issue departmental rulings that favor clients seeking to profit unethically at public expense.

2

Perks, Pork, PACs, and Other Ways to Influence Congress

Lobbyists frequently arrange personal favors called "perks" (perquisites) for congressmen, commissioners, and their chief aides. These include gifts of furniture, appliances, liquor, hotel accommodations, vacations, entertainment, cruise tickets, and expensive clothes. Lobbyists can also legally offer $2,000 speaking fees to accommodating lawmakers for speaking to business groups.

During the 1960s lobbyists flew congressmen and their staffs to free weekend vacations. Bobby Baker was secretary to the Democratic majority in the Senate. On a salary of under $20,000 a year, Baker was helped by lobbyists to accumulate over $2 million in less than nine years. He was convicted of operating get-rich schemes and accepting gifts and bribes from lobbyists for legislative favors and was sent to prison.

In addition to providing cash and "perks" for powerful legislators, lobbyists also arrange free "fact-finding" trips abroad for legislators and their major aides. In 1989 and 1990, congressmen accepted no fewer than 4,000 such trips paid for by corporation, trade group, or foreign nation lobbies.[1]

The Republicans who won both houses of Congress in the 1994 elections had made campaign promises to eliminate such perks after they were elected. But a bill to do just that was bottled up in a House committee. Lawmakers were saved the embarrassment of having to vote against it openly in order to hang on to their perks.

Senator Mitch McConnell (R-KY), who headed the Senate Ethics Committee, even introduced a new bill allowing lobbyists to continue paying for gifts to senators and their staffs and providing free vacations and entertainment.

In 1996 the House, embarrassed by media exposure of perks given to congressmen by lobbyists, set new rules prohibiting such gifts. One loophole was the exemption of gifts received "from family or friends." *Time* magazine noted, "But you can still eat well, snag the occasional case of liquor or junket to Palm Springs, California, if your friendships are sufficiently close." Or if you simply say they are.

Another loophole, *Time* pointed out, was "calling a trip a campaign event." Lawmakers also can accept travel to vacation spots by labeling these trips "for fact-finding." The Associated Press reported that in 1995 gifts to California legislators—overseas trips, tickets to sporting events and Disneyland, wining and dining—increased 55 percent over 1994.

Some impartial observers commented on the practice of paying politicians for speeches before special-interest groups. Ellen Miller, director of the Center for Responsive Politics, said, "From a special-interest point of view, it is very helpful to have a lawmaker come and speak before your group. It's another way of gaining access, and therefore influence, over a lawmaker." The problem is deciding when such well-paid speeches actually constitute special-interest bribes.[2]

Lobbyists are also expected to use their contacts to detect any impending legislation that would be detrimental to their clients,

"Our lobbyist gift ban could have a negative impact on the economy"

Congress seems to be trying to convince itself that its acceptance of food, drink, travel expenses, and fat fees for speaking are in the national interest. The public does not agree, but the power to change the laws lies in the hands of the recipients of the largess.

in order to warn the clients and give them time to prepare a lobbying effort against it by organizing mass letter-writing, phone, and e-mail campaigns to Congress opposing the legislation.[3]

The perks available from lobbyists are another reason why lawmakers usually seek reelection. "Now you have people who go to Washington, never have another job, and never come home," pointed out former Vice President Dan Quayle. "That's not good for the country, and it's one of the reasons for the cynicism voters express today."

In California advocates of limiting the terms that state legislators could serve succeeded in putting this initiative on the state ballot. However, two important Democrats—Willie Brown, then a 26-year veteran of the State Assembly, and David Roberti of the State Senate—raised more than $4 million from special-interest groups and corporations to defeat the initiative.

WINNING "PORK" FOR CLIENTS

Bills that legislate public spending on behalf of lobbyists' clients are known as "pork." Most often such pork is concealed as small amendments to a major bill.

For the four decades that the Democrats ruled Congress, their committee chairmen obliged lobbyists by passing legislation providing new dams, rail lines, electric buses, and highways. Republicans accused Democrats of buying votes with pork legislation, and promised to change things if they won control of Congress.

But in 1994, when they won Congress, 25 Republicans on the House Appropriations and House Transportation committees passed transportation spending bills costing $150 million to provide pork to corporations in their own congressional districts. President Bill Clinton threatened to veto many such Republican bills, accusing the GOP (Grand Old Party, that is, the Republicans) of bowing to "special-interest politics at its most effective and at its worst."[4]

One method used by lobbyists to get their bills passed is called "logrolling," an agreement between lawmakers to exchange support for each other's bills. A member of Congress doing their bidding will strike a deal with other members to support the lobby's bill. In exchange, that member of Congress will support the lobbyist bills that the other members want supported. For example, legislators from the Northwest might support a government subsidy for Southern tobacco growers, in exchange for support by Southern legislators for bills benefiting Western lumber companies.[5]

THE FEDERAL CORRUPT PRACTICES ACT AND OTHER ATTEMPTS AT REFORM

Bribes of legislators by lobbyists were so flagrant in 1926 that Congress passed the Federal Corrupt Practices Act. It required disclosure of campaign contributions, the amount, by whom contributed, and how it was spent. But the act was not enforced, and there were thousands of violations.

A Federal Regulation of Lobbying Act in 1946 did not restrict lobbying activity in any way. It simply required lobbyists to register and file financial reports. Many organizations were exempted from this requirement, and others found ways to evade the need to register. Many members of Congress asked lobbyists for contributions in cash, reporting only a fraction of actual receipts while pocketing the rest. It was an open scandal. In 43 years there was not a single prosecution under the act.

In 1971, Congress finally passed a new Federal Election Campaign Act to restrict campaign financing. The law was amended and strengthened in 1974 and 1976. A Federal Election Commission (FEC) was established to administer the law, affecting candidates for Congress and the White House, and political action committees (PACs), lobbies set up to support candidates or policies. The new act required disclosures and uses of funds for federal elections, provided matching public funds for presidential primary and general elections, and set limits on contributions.

Candidates are recognized as anyone raising or spending more than $5,000 in any given year of campaigning for public office. A PAC was defined as a club, committee, association, or organization that received contributions or spent more than $1,000 a year for any federal candidate. In federal elections the law prohibited direct contributions from corporations, labor organizations, and foreign nations. Cash contributions were limited to $100 per person.[6]

A serious attempt to reform lobbying took place in 1974, as a result of President Richard Nixon's forced resignation to avoid impeachment. One of the crimes of which he was accused in the Watergate scandal during his administration (1968–1974) was concealing and "laundering" millions of dollars in illegal contributions from wealthy business interests for the Nixon reelection campaign.

To "launder" illegally acquired and unreported campaign funds, they are channeled through a series of foreign banks or enterprises to make their origin difficult to trace. The lobbyists and their clients who had contributed these funds were assured favorable influence in the Nixon White House.

A newly elected 90th Congress, prodded by public outrage over the Nixon scandal, set new limits to campaign contributions from single sources. New regulations required complete disclosure of contributions made by political action committees. Those measures sought to reassure the public that by strictly limiting the money any single source could contribute to an election campaign, candidates would be free of any obligation to special interests. Nevertheless, a Supreme Court decision in *Buckley v. Valeo* removed campaign expenditure limits and further encouraged PACs. Critics were skeptical that the new congressional laws would eliminate the problem.

Each PAC was allowed to contribute up to $5,000 to a candidate's campaign in a primary (party) election, and another $5,000 for his or her general election campaign. But loopholes in the new laws let lobbyists use PACs to place ten or more times the money behind a favored candidate than the law allowed.

During the 1994 congressional elections, PACs contributed $189 million to candidates—a new record. From 1985 to 1994 the biggest PAC contributors were Banking and Finance ($56 million); Oil, Gas, Coal and Utilities ($50.4 million); Agribusiness and Food Processors ($48.9 million); Transportation Unions ($43.9 million); Insurance ($42.1 million); Real Estate ($40.6 million); Communications and Media ($37.9 million); Government Employees Unions ($37.4 million); and the Doctors, Dentists and Nurses Associations ($36.8 million).[7]

Because of public indignation, bills to end electoral corruption have been introduced and passed by each house of Congress, only to die in the committees to which they were sent for consideration. Majority parties raise more money than minority parties, so therefore those with the power to reform the system are in no hurry to do so.

HOW LEGISLATORS INFLUENCE LOBBYISTS

When Congress changed hands in 1994, many Republican legislators refused to see any lobbyists who had not contributed to their campaigns.

"Now that the Republicans control both houses of Congress," observed Richard L. Berke in *The New York Times*, "they are seeking to make up for lost time by plying what many lobby-ists and businesses describe as strong-arm tactics that are blunt by Washington standards. Many . . . Republicans are going even further to the point of dictating whom business groups should hire [as lobbyists]."[8] The preference shown by Republicans to lobbyists who contributed to their campaigns conflicted with their election oratory denouncing lobbyists as a blight on the political process. Elected Republicans made it clear that con-tributions by lobbyists and their clients were not only welcome, but expected.

It is standard practice for lawmakers from both parties to raise money from industries they regulate or legislate about. But Senator Alfonse D'Amato (R-NY), chairman of the National Republican Senatorial Committee, was rebuked by the Senate Ethics Committee in 1991 after a dozen of his activities, which involved exchanging government influence for campaign funds, had been exposed. In 1995 *Time* called him "the king of Wash-ington's money game."

He was given important fund-raising power as chairman of the Senate Banking Committee, head of Senator of Republican fund-raising for Senate candidates.

As chairman of the Senate Banking Committee, D'Amato pushed the interests of major banks and brokerages whose lob-bies had poured $1.5 million into his campaigns over the years. He secured passage of a bill for them that made it harder for investors to sue brokers who had defrauded them. His Banking Committee power enabled him to raise $14 million for Senate candidates from lobbyists.

Ann McBride, president of Common Cause, a consumer advocate organization, observed: "When the Banking chairman comes calling as the party's chief fund-raiser, and comes on in a particularly aggressive way, it isn't a scandal waiting to happen. It's a scandal right now."

D'Amato's staff solicited contributions during conversations with lobbyists about pending legislation. One lobbyist reported the aides as saying, "We're helping you, and you have to help us." Three lobbyists complained that D'Amato sought contributions from them while they had legislative business on his desk. When one such piece of legislation was held up, a D'Amato aide told the lobbyist, "Well, we haven't seen a contribution from them." The client promptly sent a $5,000 check, the lobbyist reported, and the legislation sailed through.

Common Cause found that 50 financial services, mostly banks and brokerages backing D'Amato's bills to deregulate them, contributed $600,000. By Election Day 1996, D'Amato was expected to funnel $12 million to Republican Senate candidates and $7 million to Republican state committees.

"He links money to legislation like nobody else in town," declared Donald Foley, executive director of the Democratic Senatorial Campaign Committee. "He tells donors they'd better not be giving to Democrats."[9]

In 1996, D'Amato sought to prove that Democrats were also guilty of similar acts. He chaired hearings that found that when President Clinton had been governor of Arkansas, he had allegedly bestowed political favors upon lobbyist friends who had provided campaign financing. A special investigator indicted the lobbyists, who were found guilty by a jury.

LOBBYISTS AND THE "CONTRACT WITH AMERICA"

In 1995, after the GOP had won a majority in both houses of Congress, Republican legislators met with key groups of lobbyists every week who were invited to help implement the GOP's "Contract with America," a promise of ultraconservative legislation. Those attending these meetings were known as the "Thursday Regulars." The lobbyists represented some of the nation's richest special interests. The Thursday Regulars were also joined by such conservatives as the Christian Coalition and groups lobbying for tax cuts for the wealthy.[10]

Some Republicans worried about an unfavorable reaction from voters. If their tax cuts obviously favored corporations and the wealthy, at the expense of the poor and middle class, as Democrats charged, Rep. Steve Schiff (R-NM) warned, "It will make us sitting ducks for those who argue that our party has capitulated to our [lobbying] allies." [11]

In 1994, Newt Gingrich, Speaker of a Republican-dominated House, was accused of several ethics violations. One of the violations was that of being lobbied personally by Rupert Murdoch, the media millionaire who had extensive issues before Congress. Subsequently Gingrich received a million-dollar advance to write a book for HarperCollins, a publishing house owned by Murdoch. Both Murdoch and Gingrich denied that this contract had anything to do with Murdoch's lobbying of Gingrich about his financial interests. But a media uproar compelled Gingrich to return the book advance and settle for just future royalties. One of the complaints against Speaker Gingrich was that he used his PAC committee, GOPAC, to circumvent laws limiting candidate contributions and requiring that they be made public.

When accused, Gingrich insisted that the Republican Ethics Committee alone, rather than outside counsel, should investigate the charges. Democrats referred him to his own words when House Speaker Jim Wright (D-TX) in 1989 had been accused of 69 ethics violations, many involving lobbyists. The Democrats sought to hold a committee hearing on the charges, but then Representative Newt Gingrich (R-GA) argued that the Democratic Ethics Committee would only exonerate the Democratic Speaker. He demanded the appointment of an independent counsel to investigate the charges. "The rules normally applied by the Ethics Committee to an investigation of a typical

This very cynical cartoon appears to be commenting on "honor among thieves."
The Contract with America included promises from the GOP to favor
cooperative lobbyists, but the implication here is that once the lobby money was
received, the politicians were going to be unwilling to keep their promises.

member are insufficient in an investigation of the Speaker of the House," Gingrich declared. "Clearly, this investigation has to meet a higher standard of public accountability and integrity."

Gingrich then insisted that he had broken no laws, and had nothing to fear from an impartial investigation. A subsequent investigation, however, found Gingrich guilty of violations of congressional ethics.[12]

EX-GOVERNMENT OFFICIALS TURN LOBBYISTS

When 121 displaced lawmakers left the U.S. Congress after the election of 1992, 48 became lobbyists, along with 50 top aides, and more than 30 senior government officials.[13]

A process known sarcastically in Washington as "the revolving door" allows ex-government officials to become lobbyists often for the same companies whose interests they advanced while in office. As lobbyists they are expected to make use of their former associations to influence colleagues who are still in office. Senator John McCain (R-AZ) recalled walking off the Senate floor with a former Senate colleague. "Next thing I know," McCain complained, "he's lobbying me hard."[14]

When former Representative Lloyd Meeds (D-WA) left Capitol Hill in 1979, like many ex-legislators he hired out as a lobbyist for special interests, at first for Alaskan hospitals. Stung by widespread criticism of lobbyists, he protested, "People think lobbyists work only for big industries. But there's good lobbying and bad lobbying." Having made this point, Meeds then became a lobbyist for a big power company seeking to slash the price it had to pay for electricity.

Michael Deaver, a major aide to President Ronald Reagan, turned lobbyist when he left the Reagan administration. He won special privileges from his friends in office for TWA, Boeing, and other large corporations. In December 1987 he was convicted of perjury in testifying about his lobbying activities, was fined $100,000, placed on probation for three years, and forbidden to lobby the federal government for profit.

Often ex-cabinet members become lobbyists, like James Watt, former Secretary of the Interior in the Reagan administration. He lobbied Samuel Pierce, Secretary of the Department of Housing and Urban Development (HUD), on behalf of several contractors seeking government funding for their projects. Brought before Congress, and then a grand jury, to testify about those dealings, Watt lied and was indicted for perjury.

David Rubenstein, a young staff member in the Carter White House, became a lobbyist after President Jimmy Carter lost his bid for reelection. He soon quit, however, shocked by the pressure for campaign funds put on lobbyists by lawmakers. "I found it demeaning," he related. "It was legalized bribery. You'd go up to talk to a senator and the minute you got back to your office the phone would be ringing and it would be the senator's aide asking when you might be able to throw a fund-raiser."[15]

Former Senator Warren Rudman (R-NH), who refused to turn lobbyist when he left office in 1992, estimated that even ex-lawmakers who are only "moderately successful" at lobbying earn between $250,000 and $400,000, or twice to three times what they were paid as congressmen. That's a powerful incentive to go through the "revolving door."[16]

By 1978, Congress passed an Ethics in Government Act, which required a cooling-off period before certain ex-government officials could lobby their former agencies. But there were so many loopholes in the law as it was written that Representative Bob Eckhardt (D-TX) scoffed, "It's one of those apparent reforms that is not a reform at all."

Because of the big money earned by lobbyists, their numbers doubled from 1982 to 1992. By the mid-1990s, an estimated 80,000 known lobbyists were practicing in Washington.[17]

3

Lobbying the White House
and State Legislatures

"Public opinion shows that a majority of Americans feel that lobbyists are the real power in Washington," declared Senator Carl Levin (D-MI) in 1995. "Only 22 percent believes it's the president. We must act to restore confidence that in fact their representatives control the power in Washington."

One might imagine that lobbyists would not dare lobby the president or his aides, or that those high officials would be above dealing with lobbyists. But examples from American history prove the opposite.

When Ulysses S. Grant was president (1869–1877), his brother-in-law Abel Rathbone Corbin became a paid lobbyist for Jay Gould and Jim Fisk, speculators determined to corner the gold market. Corbin persuaded President Grant to announce that all government obligations would henceforth be paid in gold. Meanwhile Gould and Fisk had almost entirely cornered the gold market, which soared on Grant's announcement. When he learned of the scheme, Grant angrily ordered the U.S. Treasury to flood the open market with $4 million in gold, which caused the price of gold to plunge, ruining the dismayed speculators.[1]

Harry S. Truman (1945–1953) was also victimized by lobbyists. A lobbyist named John Maragon gave gifts of freezers, expensive furs, and perfumes to Truman's friend and military aide, Harry Vaughn, to distribute among the president's inti-mates. Vaughn let Maragon use the White House to influence the award of lucrative government contracts to his clients, who paid Maragon 5 percent. When the press exposed this scan-dal, jubilant Republicans denounced the Democratic Truman regime as corrupt. Lobbyist Maragon went to jail.[2]

A similar lobbyist bribery scandal erupted in the adminis-tration of President Dwight Eisenhower (1953–1961). Sherman Adams, the president's chief aide, was lobbied by textile tycoon Bernard Goldfine, who had contributed to Adams's past politi-cal campaigns for governor of New Hampshire.

Goldfine was in trouble with the Federal Trade Commission (FTC) for falsely labeling his wool products. He gave Adams expensive suits and vicuna overcoats, liquor, and furnishings, and paid for his hotel and resort bills. Adams ordered the FTC to call off its investigation of Goldfine.

But when Goldfine committed more violations of the law, the FTC decided to crack down. Once again Adams tried to get the agency to squash the investigation, but the public learned that President Eisenhower himself had received one of Gold-fine's expensive vicuna coats. The press demanded that Adams be fired. After congressional hearings, Goldfine was sentenced to jail, and Adams resigned.

Government commissions, official agencies appointed by the White House, are prime targets of lobbyists because they are entrusted with the enforcement of the laws that Congress has passed. Supposedly they are the watchdogs of the public.

"The people don't know that these commissions are an arm of Congress," said Speaker Sam Rayburn (D-TX) in 1955. "They do what we don't have time to do. Yet Eisenhower has taken over and even appoints his friends. If you have a good law and appoint bad administrators, you just about kill the law. That is what Eisenhower is doing today."

This 1885 cartoon depicts Jay Gould literally in the role of his nickname—the pirate of Wall Street.

During the Eisenhower administration, an investigation revealed that five of the seven commissioners on the Federal Communications Commission (FCC) allowed lobbyists for the industries they regulated to pay their travel, restaurant, entertainment, and vacation expenses. At the same time the commissioners billed the government for these expenses. The lobbyists also provided the commissioners with free television sets.

Professor Bernard Schwartz of New York University was appointed chief counsel for congressional hearings on this lobbying scandal. He called for public hearings in which the commissioners would be required to disclose these gifts and who provided them. The investigating committee's ranking Republican angrily denounced Schwartz's plan as "a lousy thing to do."[3]

Several scandals involving lobbying also erupted during the Nixon administration. A loan of $205,000 was made by a lobbyist for the Hughes Tool Company to F. Donald Nixon, the president's brother, to save his business from bankruptcy. The loan was never repaid. Soon afterward millionaire Howard Hughes was granted new routes for his TWA airline to fly; a Justice Department suit against his tool company was settled; his aircraft company was awarded defense contracts; and his tool company received business from the Civil Aeronautics Board, which it had been unable to obtain before the loan to F. Donald Nixon.[4]

When E. I. Du Pont de Nemours wanted a law reducing the tax on capital gains on General Motors stock, the corporation hired presidential confidant Clark Gifford as its lobbyist. Gifford won audiences for Crawford H. Greenewalt, president of Du Pont, with more than 50 Democratic members of Congress and top government officials. The law that Du Pont wanted was easily passed.

When Ronald Reagan ran for the White House in 1980, he was accused of being in the pocket of right-wing extremists because he had accepted campaign contributions from the lobbyist for the right-wing John Birch Society.[5]

Susan Thomases, a close friend of President Bill Clinton and his wife, Hillary, used her friendship as a lobbyist for a group of Puerto Rican companies in a dispute with a government agency. She also lobbied for J. R. Morgan and Company to win government approval for Morgan to buy and control Russia's nuclear weapons stockpile.

Newsweek correspondent Michael Isikoff reported one participant in Thomases's deals as observing, "There's no question Susan used the spectre of White House interest as her calling card." During a meeting with officials resisting her lobbying, Thomases hinted darkly that after a Clinton administration reorganization, "Who knows where you're all going to end up?"[6]

The prestige of ex-presidents is a target of lobbyists for foreign countries, who offer rich compensations for visits to and speeches in their countries. When George Bush left the White House, he was paid a large sum by a lobby for the so-called Woman's Federation for World Peace, set up by the Reverend Sun Myung Moon's Unification Church, a controversial religious cult, to speak in Tokyo on "family values."[7]

Perhaps the most incredible type of federal lobbying occurs when government agencies themselves spend taxpayers' dollars lobbying for their own preservation. One example was the office of the Small Business Administration (SBA), which issued 12-page instruction manuals to lobbyists on which lawmakers to pressure, and coaching congressmen on what to write, to save their agency. The National Federation of Independent Businessmen obliged by keeping the $6 million government department from being cut out of the budget.

LOBBYING STATE LEGISLATURES

Lobbying state legislatures for private profit is an old American tradition. In 1824 many companies lobbied state legislatures for land grants to build canals. Often these companies were run by unscrupulous operators who delayed the work as long as possible, then blackmailed more money out of the legislatures to complete their projects.

The growth of big corporations following the Civil War led lobbyists to bribe state legislators to vote in favor of subsidies for railroad, oil, coal, and timber companies. "I think I can say, and say with pride," Mark Twain observed dryly, "that we have legislatures that bring higher prices than any in the world."

Corporate lobbies exercise even greater power in state legislatures than they do in Congress. They can push their bills into law much more easily and cheaply. State legislatures tend to meet infrequently and briefly, because the salaries paid are generally so low that legislators must maintain businesses or careers during their terms in office. Often, in their haste to adjourn sessions, they rush through bills by voice vote—bills they have scarcely read, let alone studied. Many of these bills are written for state legislators by the lobbyists who bribe them with campaign funds.

In 1906 lobbyists for oil companies, railroads, banks, and utilities sat in the back rooms of the Texas legislature where decisions were made. They roamed freely on the floor of the legislature, often sitting at legislators' desks and even casting votes on behalf of absent legislators. Lobbyists bought their influence with cash, as well as paying for meals, hotel bills, trips, and prostitutes for legislators.

Philadelphia reporter Bernard McCormick once noted that in the Pennsylvania legislature, the lobbyist for Sun Oil was "often referred to as the fifty-first senator," and the lobbyist for Penn Central Railroad was "considered the fifty-second." Former Senator Joseph S. Clark (D-PA) declared, "I have no hesitation in stating my deep conviction that the legislatures of America . . . are presently the greatest menace to . . . the successful operation of the democratic process."

Although many states have passed laws against water pollution, these laws have been highly ineffectual. State funds to help local communities control water pollution were negligible. In one third of the states, not a single polluter was brought to court between 1956 and 1961 because their lobbyists were too powerful.

"Instead of being 'closer to the people,'" observed Maxwell S. Stewart, former secretary of the Public Affairs Committee, "state and local governments often seem to be controlled by cliques and factions that are insensitive to the needs of their poorer residents. Experience seems to show that some disadvantaged people—children, the aged, disabled, blind, and other handicapped persons—arouse sufficient national sympathy and support for Congress to vote funds for their specific needs. But in state houses and city halls these same groups cannot compete with vested interests like the road-building or tax lobbies."

At the same time it is easier for lobbyists to pass legislation to fight fraud and other criminal activites in state houses than in Congress. In an article titled "Workers' Compensation: A License to Steal," in *the Reader's Digest* of December 1992, Dale Van Atta revealed that, from 1984 to 1987, Oregon had the highest frequency of compensation claims of any state, with one in four estimated to be fraudulent.

This high percentage of insurance fraud meant that the insurance companies had to charge much higher rates for coverage. An insurance company lobby, aided by Governor Neil Goldschmidt, publicized outrageous cases that infuriated the public. The Oregon legislature was prodded into passing an antifraud program in 1990. Undercover and surveillance units were set up. After this crackdown, rejected claims rose from 12 percent to 29 percent, and the number of claims filed fell by 29 percent.

By 1971, however, many state legislatures had been so corrupted by lobbyists that in New Jersey a new U.S. district attorney, Herbert J. Stern, brought no fewer than 61 high state and city officials to trial for bribery, conspiracy, extortion, tax evasion, mail fraud, and perjury. "The same things are going on in other states," Stern declared. "They just don't get caught."

By that time, most Americans had become suspicious of state legislatures, characterizing them, according to reporter Bernard McCormick, as "a bunch of thieves." In April 1973 a Rutgers University survey found that three of four Americans polled believed that their local government was corrupt.

During the 1970s a Citizens Conference on State Legislatures made a study of them and evaluated them in order of excellence. At the top of the list then, rated from one to ten, were California, New York, Illinois, Florida, Wisconsin, Iowa, Hawaii, Michigan, Nebraska, and Minnesota.

The ten worst, in order, were Alabama, Wyoming, Delaware, North Carolina, Arkansas, Georgia, South Carolina, Arizona, Mississippi, and Montana.

In 1983, March Fong Eu, secretary of state of California, warned that if the legislature didn't act to control "the unbelievable spending that is turning elections into auctions," she would introduce a citizens' initiative to control campaign spending. She pointed out that lobbyists had raised an incredible $150 million to spend on California's 1982 elections.

In July 1989 the Texas Senate deliberated over legislation favoring Texas chicken processor Lonnie Pilgrim. During the debate Pilgrim passed out personal checks with the payee's name left blank to 9 of the 31 state senators, stating they were campaign contributions. "It would be difficult to make it into a bribery case," observed Travis County district attorney Ronnie Earle. "In Texas, it's almost impossible to bribe a public official as long as you report it." The rewards collected by lobbyists for their efforts were bountiful. The top lobbyist firm, Carpenter, Snodgrass & Associates, earned 1993 fees of $2,270,000.

In 1995 the state that was once listed as having the best legislature fell in disfavor with its voters. By a 2-to-1 margin, voters polled by the *Los Angeles Times* described themselves as "angry" with the lawmakers in Sacramento, whom they viewed as serving only a few big special interests. Respect for the Senate and Assembly sank so low that 75 percent of those polled said they trusted their county governments more than they did the state legislature. *Los Angeles Times* poll director John Brennan observed that the poll results revealed "an increasing tide of cynicism on the part of the public toward state government."

HOW A STATE LOBBY OPERATES

1. Big corporate lobbyists are invited to a fundraiser for a major election candidate.
2. At the fund-raiser, the lobbyists give or pledge campaign funds to the candidate.
3. Often the lobbyist will contribute campaign funds to both rival candidates, so that no matter which one wins the lobbyist will have access to the elected state official.
4. When the candidate wins, he or she is visited by the lobbyist who provided campaign funds with a proposed bill that will benefit the lobbyist's client.
5. The elected lawmaker then proposes the legislation and tries to round up votes for it, often by pledging to vote for other lawmakers' bills in return.
6. If the bill is passed by the state legislature, it is usually signed by the governor and becomes state law. Often whatever a lobbyist's client spends in campaign contributions pays off in enormous profits made possible by this bought-and-paid-for legislation.

California topped the list of the ten best state legislatures in America during the 1970s. Perhaps this cartoon showing a Los Angeles judge ruling against the 1974 California Political Reform Act designed to restrict the activities of lobbyists provides the answer to why California citizens no longer trust their state government.

On the other hand, lobbies opposed to what they consider excessive federal wielding of power have convinced many lawmakers to vote against it. Charles Reese reports in the *Conservative Chronicle* of July 10, 1996, that a new group called the Southern League has been lobbying hard for "self-government, state sovereignty, ordered liberty in the tradition of Christianity and Western civilization." The lobbying of this and other states' rights advocates has pressured Congress to strip the federal government of many of its powers and return them to the states. They influenced the passage of such bills as the Welfare Reform Act of 1996, giving states the power to regulate welfare.

The Democrats warned that turning this power over to the states would hurt children of the poor, since each state would be free to cut welfare funds as much as it wished. Republicans argued that governors would have a better knowledge of local welfare cases, with the ability to curb welfare payments to nonworking teenage mothers living on their own, and to those ablebodied persons who prefer to be supported by taxpayers instead of taking a job.

President Clinton had qualms about some provisions of the new law, but signed the bill, aware that the antiwelfare lobby had convinced most Americans that it was necessary.

4

The Powerful Oil, Tobacco, and Firearms Lobbies

The original mastermind of the oil industry was John D. Rockefeller, owner of the Standard Oil Company. In the late 1870s he secretly negotiated midnight contracts to form a trust with the nation's 15 largest oil refiners.

The public grew indignant when reporters revealed the unscrupulous methods that Rockefeller had used to force companies out of business for refusing to buy from Standard Oil. In 1879 he and others in the trust were indicted for criminal conspiracy "to secure a monopoly of the oil industry, to oppress other refiners . . . to fraudulently control prices."

When Ohio courts ordered his trust dissolved, Rockefeller simply reincorporated it as a holding company under accommodating laws that his lobbyists had passed for him in New Jersey. By 1900 he had eliminated all major competitors and amassed a tremendous fortune. His lobbyists made sure that Congress tolerated the oil monopoly that was detested by the public. Theodore Roosevelt responded to public anger by introducing some antitrust legislation, but as Thomas Bailey notes in his book *Presidential Greatness,* "As a trust-buster he was something of a 'bust'; at best, the trusts were only temporarily curbed." In 1914, President Woodrow Wilson forced Congress to pass the

Clayton Anti-Trust Act. Ironically, big business saw to it that this act was distorted to outlaw labor strikes as "restraint of interstate commerce."

During the administration of President Warren Harding (1921–1923) a great oil scandal erupted as a result of the bribery of Secretary of the Interior Albert B. Fall by oil tycoon Harry Sinclair, who had given Fall more than $300,000. In return Fall secretly leased to Sinclair the government's oil reserve at Teapot Dome, Wyoming, and other sites as well. When a newsman dug up the story in 1923, Fall was forced to resign in a scandal that gave a black eye to the Harding administration. Fall was convicted of accepting bribes, fined $100,000, and sent to jail for a year.[1]

In 1941 the oil lobby contributed $25,000 in unrecorded cash to help elect Lyndon B. Johnson (D-TX) to the Senate. He became the channel through which oil lobby money flowed to Democratic legislators, who could be counted on to vote favorably on bills benefiting the oil industry.

Thanks to the powerful oil lobby in Congress, oilmen enjoyed all the advantages of a trust. Congressmen who were in the oil lobby's pockets voted to award oil companies a 27.5 percent tax depletion allowance, permitting oilmen to exempt that much of their income from federal taxation.

Senator Paul Douglas (D-IL) pointed out that some oil companies had net incomes of more than $12 million and escaped paying even a cent in taxes. Some even received a half-million-dollar tax credit from the federal government.

The oil lobby was as powerful in the states as in Congress. Robert W. Calvert, chairman of the Democratic State Executive Committee in Texas, declared in 1947: "The oil industry today is in complete control of the state government and state politics." Ronnie Dugger, contributing editor of the *Texas Observer,* noted: "The rich think they can buy stock in the legislature or an executive agency as they can in a corporation, and they can."

A 1922 cartoon showing Washington officials racing down an oil-slicked road to the White House, trying desperately to outpace the Teapot Dome scandal.

The oil lobby carefully studied a 1947 Supreme Court decision that although Washington did not own the states' offshore lands, which held valuable oil deposits in the continental shelf, the federal government nevertheless had the right to protect the nation's coastlines. To get around this decision, the oil lobby pressured Congress to pass a "states' rights" bill that would give each state the right to lease its own tidelands.

"It's not a matter of states' rights," charged Secretary of the Interior Harold L. Ickes, "but the issue of the rights of certain oil companies to take oil from the states because it's easier. Those who are backing bills to continue state ownership are raising the cry 'Stop thief' in order to let the oil companies get away with murder."

Soon after President Eisenhower's election in 1953, big-business interests, anxious to exploit tidelands oil deposits, lobbied Congress into giving states the title to the submerged lands off their coasts.

The oil lobby also succeeded in getting a bill through Congress for a government commission to remove federal controls from the price of natural gas. Price increases would extract about $1 billion a year in extra profits from homeowners. President Eisenhower was so shocked by what he denounced as "arrogant" lobbying that he vetoed the oil lobby bill.

When Richard Nixon became president, the oil lobby won restrictions on foreign oil imports, inflicting higher gas and home-heating-fuel prices on Americans. Senator William Proxmire (D-WI) observed, "The consumers have been sacrificed once again to the interests of big oil."

The New York Times charged that the Nixon administration, which prided itself on "trimming outlays for health, education and welfare, does not mind letting consumers pay out more than $60 billion in oil bills over the coming decade."

Over the outraged opposition of conservationists, the oil lobby also won passage of a bill to build an Alaskan oil pipeline across the ecologically sensitive tundra.

In September 1973 the attorneys general of all the states met in an angry conference to demand that Congress break up the oil monopoly. Six filed state suits against the oil companies. Representative Les Aspin (D-WI) accused the Nixon administration of letting oil companies get away with making huge profits by using the Arab-Israeli war as a pretext for falsely claiming an oil shortage in Middle East imports and raising prices. Aspin noted that the oil lobby had contributed $5 million to the president's reelection campaign in 1972. "After their massive contributions," Aspin said wryly, "there is little he can do to control them."

All over the country long lines of cars were forced to wait at service stations. There were fights and threats when stations ran out of oil with cars still in line. The oil lobby told consumers that there was a chronic oil shortage, which consumer critics charged was deliberately arranged. Many independent gas stations selling cheaper fuel were forced out of business when the major oil companies rationed deliveries, while raising prices in the gas stations they controlled and serviced.

Americans were enraged, demanding that the oil company monopoly be broken up and oil profits be heavily taxed. When the alleged oil shortage was declared over, however, and consumers were once more able to get all the gas they needed at reasonable prices, they forgot the hardships inflicted upon them by the oil monopoly, which remained intact.

Environmentalists demanded that offshore oil rigs be banned within 3 miles (5 kilometers) of all U.S. coasts, especially after an oil rig near Santa Barbara, California, began spilling oil uncontrollably in 1969, fouling 40 miles (64 kilometers) of beaches, destroying sea life, killing seabirds, and soiling thousands of small boats. Public anger was so great that Congress was forced to hold hearings about ways to prevent such spills from oil rigs and tankers in the future. Environmental organizations sent lobbyists to testify and demand tighter laws against spillage. They also publicized these views widely in the media, and hundreds of angry letters poured into lawmakers' offices.

But the oil lobbies made sure that Congress turned deaf ears to any limitation of offshore oil rigs. In 1973, Congress also indicated its readiness to pass a Nixon administration bill to build new superports to accommodate oil supertankers in any coastal state, whether or not the state wanted one.

New Jersey Governor William T. Cahill, whose state was heavily dependent upon its beach resort industry, denounced the bill as "an environmental nightmare." Other governors of coastal states, energized by voter indignation, also protested vigorously, and the bill was shelved.

In 1995 when the Republicans controlled Congress, the Democrats charged that they had ceded too much influence to oil lobbyists by inviting them into internal planning sessions, even allowing them to draft legislation beneficial to oil interests. Oil lobbyists also sought to have Congress permit tapping the reserves of the oil-rich Arctic National Wildlife Refuge, whose 1.5 million acres (600,000 hectares) were off-limits to drilling. A *Time* magazine poll showed 67 percent of the public opposed. To thwart the oil lobby, President Bill Clinton threatened a veto and contemplated declaring the Refuge a national monument, making it immune to exploitation. Public opposition to an oil invasion of the Refuge was so great that Congress did not dare pass the bill.[2]

In April and May 1996, Americans were shocked when oil prices at gas stations suddenly shot up as much as 40 cents a gallon. The oil lobby gave all kinds of excuses for it, primarily blaming short supplies and increased demand. But this time, its fat campaign contributions would not stave off a Justice Department investigation of possible collusion by the oil companies that had abruptly raised oil prices the same amount simultaneously.

Congress also responded by hastily promising hearings on the price rises that were outraging the public.

Seeking to capitalize on that outrage, the Republican Congress swiftly introduced a bill to repeal the 4.3-cent gas tax, which would supposedly reduce the price at the gas pump.

THE TOBACCO LOBBY

The earliest scientific study of the effects of cigarette smoking on health were made as early as 1937 by Dr. Raymond Pearl, head biologist at Johns Hopkins University. He reported to the New York Academy of Medicine that in 7,000 cases of persons aged 30 to 60 studied, 61 percent more heavy smokers died than nonsmokers. But almost all the media, which derived over $50 million a year from tobacco company advertising, suppressed Dr. Pearl's report.

The first crusader against the tobacco lobby was journalist George Seldes in 1940. "I started the campaign against smoking," he told me, "and lived to see a national law against it. . . . I know no big newspaper which takes tobacco advertising which published the medical report that one third of all deaths, that is, 100,000 lung cancer deaths per year, are due to smoking."[3]

During the administrations of Presidents John F. Kennedy and Lyndon B. Johnson, medical evidence that cigarette smoking led to cancer and heart disease forced the tobacco companies to stop advertising on TV and to label cigarette packages and print ads with health warnings.

In April 1994 top executives of the cigarette industry were called before a congressional hearing to answer charges that they had increased levels of nicotine in their cigarettes to make them more addictive. They testified that they did not believe nicotine was addictive and had not tried to make cigarettes addictive. They also denied allegations that cigarettes caused cancer or heart disease, responsible for 400,000 U.S. deaths a year, and adding some $68 billion to national health care costs.

But a year later the Justice Department secured documents revealing the companies' own research on nicotine. These proved that the tobacco executives knew as early as 1969 that the craving created by tobacco was so powerful that cigarettes would even "pre-empt food in times of scarcity on the smoker's priority list." One company report described nicotine as "a potent drug."

Food and Drug Administration Commissioner David Kessler announced that the FDA would consider trying to regulate cigarettes as an addictive drug. The tobacco lobby moved swiftly to pull congressional strings to block that move. It insisted that the tobacco company documents did not reflect actual tobacco industry policy.

Representative Martin T. Meehan (D-MA) urged Attorney General Janet Reno to convene a grand jury to investigate possible perjury charges against the tobacco executives for their testimony in Congress.[4]

In 1995 two new studies showed an alarming increase in smoking by young people. Tobacco lobbyists rushed to stiffen congressional opposition to a bill by Representative Meehan to raise the cigarette tax from $.24 to $1.98 to discourage teenage smoking.

President Clinton suggested that he might drop efforts to regulate nicotine as a drug if the tobacco industry agreed to spend $150 million a year in a campaign against teenage smoking. Meanwhile the industry was spending more than $400 million a year for cigarette advertising, much of it targeted at teenagers.

The tobacco lobby denounced the president's requirement, however, as "an illegal tax."

The Republican Congress was reluctant to pass any legislation opposed by tobacco lobbyists, who had contributed almost six times more money to their campaigns than had been contributed to the Democrats.

A federal inspector general found that teens could easily buy cigarettes anywhere in the country, even in states that banned cigarette sales to minors. President Clinton called smoking a "pediatric disease" on the order of polio and smallpox, and vowed to cut smoking by some 3 million minors by 2002. He turned over tobacco regulation to the FDA, which issued new rules forbidding advertising targeted at minors; prohibited vending-machine and mail-order sales; banned cigarette sales to youths under the age of 18; and banned tobacco sponsorship of, and billboard advertising at, sporting events.

"The FDA," fumed House Speaker Newt Gingrich, who had benefited from tobacco lobby funds, "has lost its mind!"

Tobacco lobbyists immediately condemned the president's action as an outrageous abuse of government power. They denounced FDA Commissioner David Kessler as the leader of "an anti-smoking cabal" inside his agency. The industry filed suit in North Carolina challenging the FDA's jurisdiction over tobacco. The advertising industry also filed suit, claiming that the FDA regulations curbing TV advertising of cigarettes to teens violated the First Amendment guarantees of freedom of speech and freedom of the press.

Tobacco lobbyists insisted that the industry did not seek to induce teenagers to smoke. But documents from the industry's files, and a new study in the *Journal of the National Cancer Institute,* proved that as early as 1973 the industry was seeking ways to reach young potential smokers.

A California study of more than 3,500 teenagers found that those who were receptive to ads, or who wanted tobacco industry premiums, were four times more likely to take up smoking than those who were led to smoke by peer pressure.

The tobacco lobby then sought to head off the administration's war on teen smoking by announcing that the industry would initiate its own $20 million campaign to discourage it, and would also label cigarette packs "Underage Sale Prohibited."

That did not satisfy the president. "It is wrong as well as illegal to hook one million children a year on tobacco," he insisted, and pointed out that studies showed that 9 out of 10 smokers became addicted before the age of 21.[5]

The American Medical Association also fought the tobacco lobby by pushing to have tobacco regulated by the government as an addictive drug. AMA President Dr. Lonnie Bristow compared the tobacco lobby to the Medellin drug cartel—the international ring that was producing, smuggling, and distributing cocaine and other hard drugs. He declared that its hiding of scientific data proving smoking injurious was "the most despicable action by an industry I had ever heard."

Polls showed that President Clinton's program for cracking down on the tobacco industry's advertising to teens had widespread public support. The tobacco lobby fought back with arguments that the industry's ads were aimed only at promoting brands to people who already smoked. But in a poll taken by the Associated Press, 75 percent of people supported the president's demand that the tobacco industry try to discourage teen smoking. Even 65 percent of smokers supported that plan.

Tobacco lobbyists let it be known that in the elections of 1996, Clinton would lose voters in all the Southern tobacco-producing states. Representative Charles Rose (D-NC) urged the president to soften antismoking measures. Nevertheless, Clinton did win a second term in office, despite opposition from the tobacco lobby.

Voters were indignant that the government provided subsidies to tobacco growers, while condemning smoking as an unhealthy habit. The subsidy was a reward to tobacco lobbyists who had helped finance the election campaigns of many lawmakers. During the 1990s tobacco PAC lobbies made sure that Congress did

When threatened with antismoking legislation, the tobacco lobby has not been shy about flexing its muscle, especially with Republican members of the Senate and House who had accepted major campaign contributions from the industry.

little or nothing to regulate tobacco by pouring $16.7 million into influencing Washington. When bills were introduced to kill tobacco subsidies, two dozen lobbyists from the tobacco states met in the office of House majority leader Dick Armey (R-TX) to demand that the bills be killed by being kept off the House floor.

The tobacco lobby is so powerful in Congress that many political observers doubt that any antismoking measures will reduce teen smoking significantly—no more than the "dangerous to your health" warnings on cigarette packs have stopped addicted adults from continuing to smoke.[6]

The tobacco lobby was furious at the TV media for what it considered prejudiced reporting of the tobacco controversy. Philip Morris filed a lawsuit against ABC-TV for stating that the company deliberately added nicotine from outside sources to its cigarettes to addict smokers. ABC-TV apologized for the statement about "outside sources," but still maintained that the company did control the nicotine levels to addict smokers. Philip Morris accepted the half-apology and called off its lawsuit.[7]

In 1996, as more and more links between cigarette smoking and disease—heart attacks, emphysema, and cancer—were reported, many states began filing suit against the tobacco companies to recover millions of dollars spent in treating smoking-related diseases. Antismoking lobbies widely circulated *The New York Times* report that tobacco addiction was killing at least 425,000 Americans a year.

THE FIREARMS LOBBY

The United States has about 40,000 firearms-related deaths a year, the highest in the world. The National Rifle Association (NRA) started a PAC in 1977. By 1986 it was distributing $4.8 million to state and federal candidates for office. Almost $1 million went to lawmakers who had voted for the NRA lobby's

The National Rifle Association has been a powerful influence on legislators, a situation spoofed in this Renault cartoon showing Congress dancing to the lobby's compelling tune.

position opposing the ban on interstate sale of handguns. The NRA lobby has contributed heavily to legislators' campaign funds, assuring the defeat of efforts to pass tough gun-control laws.

The powerful lobby has the ability to flood Congress with mail, e-mail, and phone calls from 3 million members opposing gun-control measures. Its bloc vote amounting to as much as 4 percent of votes cast can swing elections, and often does. This power is not lost on candidates for national, state, and county offices.

The NRA bases its opposition to gun control on the Second Amendment: "A well regulated Militia, being necessary to the security of a free State, the right of the people to keep and bear Arms, shall not be infringed." Opponents of the NRA argue that this amendment provides for a "well regulated militia" to bear arms, not for individuals to do so.

In 1980, Representative Peter Rodino (D-NJ), chairman of the House Judiciary Committee, bottled up an NRA bill passed by the Senate, calling it "dead on arrival." NRA lobbyist James Jay Baker simply shrugged and said that he would wait for the bill's "resurrection."

That year Rodino joined Senator Ted Kennedy (D-MA) in pushing a bill that threatened owners of unlicensed handguns with a year in jail. The NRA lobby denounced the bill as also threatening owners of hunting rifles and pistols for target practice. The lobby made sure that the bill was killed in committee.

The NRA lobby heavily publicized the fact that President Ronald Reagan, a lifelong NRA member, also opposed gun-control legislation, even after an assassination attempt on his life. Many lawmakers hesitated to pass such legislation because of the NRA lobby's insistence that gun ownership was necessary to protect homes and families against urban crime.

"If one of these wavering members is uncertain about the feelings in his home district," lobbyist Baker explains, "we fly in one or two people from the district—usually people who own gun shops—to talk to him."

In 1981 the NRA lobby provided $85,000 in contributions to members of the Senate Judiciary Committee. One year later that committee approved a bill making it easier to buy and sell guns. When Republicans won control of Congress in 1994, they went even further by telling the lobbyists who wanted to meet with them to hire only Republican lobbyists.[8]

In 1995 the Republicans' House Reform and Oversight Committee held hearings on a 1993 federal raid to search for an arsenal allegedly stacked at the Branch Davidian compound near Waco, Texas. The raid ended with the compound going up in flames with men, women, and children inside.

Speaker Gingrich loaded the committee with legislators indebted to the NRA. "They [the NRA and the Republicans] planned the whole hearings together," accused Representative Charles E. Schumer (D-NY). "The hearings, from the beginning, had an odor to them, and to me it's very clear that the NRA is the skunk."

Tammy Begun, a lobbyist for the NRA, was allowed to sit with the committee's staff at the hearings. NRA lobbyists also gathered evidence for the hearings, coordinated by an NRA lawyer who also represented gun importers involved in a dispute with the Bureau of Alcohol, Tobacco and Firearms.

Tanya Metaksa, the NRA's chief lobbyist, declared that the NRA's role in the hearings was no different from that played by other interested groups. But Tammy Begun abandoned her staff seat when her right to be there was questioned by reporters.

The NRA sent out a fund-raising letter calling the federal agents involved in the Branch Davidian raid "jackbooted government thugs." Former President George Bush quit the NRA, declaring himself offended by the letter. Police Commissioner Richard L. Judd of New Britain, Connecticut, also resigned in protest. The NRA lost over 300,000 members, almost a tenth of the total.

President Bill Clinton strongly criticized the NRA lobby as a special-interest group that dictated to Congress while endangering public safety and the police by opposing gun control. The NRA assailed the president as a "grave threat" to the right to bear arms. But polls showed that most Americans favored gun control. Clinton charged that Republican support of the NRA marked them as "political extremists."[9]

A gun-control bill was fought bitterly in Congress following an assassination attempt on the life of President Ronald Reagan in 1981, which severely crippled his press secretary James Brady. Brady and his wife Sarah lobbied against the gun lobby for a dozen years, testifying in congressional hearings, urging for a gun-control bill named after him. It provided a five-day waiting period for gun purchases, and a national computer network to check the backgrounds of gun buyers. President Clinton signed the Brady Bill into law in 1993 despite angry protests from the NRA.

Bob Dole (R-KS), Senate majority leader, wrote the NRA in 1995 saying that he would sponsor the repeal of this ban, insisting that "disarming law-abiding citizens only places them at the mercy of those who break the law."[10]

After several incidents in which semiautomatic weapons were used to slaughter large numbers of people, an outraged public and the antigun lobby pressured Congress into banning the manufacture and sale of 19 models of such weapons. Stiff lobbying by the NRA forced a close Senate vote—51 for the ban, 49 against. NRA Executive Vice President Wayne La Pierre grimly warned the lawmakers, "We have a real long memory!" This translated to: If you voted for the ban on automatic weapons, don't come to us for campaign funds!

Money from the NRA lobby continued to flow to Capitol Hill. The freshmen Republican members elected to the House in 1994 received $720,000 in NRA campaign contributions. House Speaker Newt Gingrich assured the NRA's chief lobbyist that no gun-control legislation would move through the House as long as he remained Speaker.[11]

5

Environmental Issues: The Lobbies that Fight For and Against Them

In this country chemicals in the air cripple Florida cattle, peel paint on Maine homes and cars, kill California pines, and ruin orchards in Texas and Illinois.

"Americans are paying billions of dollars each year as the price of contaminated air," declared John D. Middleton, former commissioner of the National Air Pollution Control Administration. Worse, large numbers of Americans suffer from respiratory ailments as a result of air pollution.

"Americans are feeling the squeeze in our impacted cities, our choking highways, our disfigured land," said former Secretary of the Interior Stewart L. Udall. "We feel it in power failures and water shortages; in smog and sewage and slums. . . . Our rivers and lakes are open sewers; emphysema is claiming lives at an alarming rate; and noise has damaged the hearing of three out of five men. We suicidally abuse our environment—by our numbers, our affluence, our technology."

Lobbyists for the chemical companies and polluting factories fight legislation to protect the environment. Lumber companies try to harvest trees in state and national forests. Real estate developers seek to clear wooded lands. Mining companies practice landscape-destroying strip mining. Power companies defend the pollution they cause as necessary because of the nation's great need for energy.

Sometimes a lobby has such enormous popular support that it doesn't need to contribute campaign funds to win legislative support. Such was the case with a youth lobby called Environmental Action, Inc., which organized "Earth Day" on April 22, 1970, to dramatize the perils of pollution.

More than 20 U.S. senators and many governors participated, aware that by doing so they would win votes as protectors of the environment. Congress responded to public pressure by establishing a new federal Environmental Protection Agency (EPA), with the power to establish national quality standards for air and water to protect the public health. But by 1973 big-business lobbies saw to it that legislators yielded to pressures to relax antipollution regulations. Power companies and big plants were once more permitted to burn air-polluting sulfurous coal. New areas of coal deposits were opened to strip mining, which destroyed landscapes. Preparations were made to drill for oil off American beaches, even in nature preserves. The lobbies also made it easier for legislators to vote for tolerating pollution by its propaganda warning that the public would otherwise suffer fuel shortages for cars and homes.

The Republican Congress passed a bill in November 1994 cutting the EPA budget by a sixth and making deep reductions in aid to states for water-pollution control and EPA enforcement.

Aware of growing public criticism, the House voted down a bill that business lobbies wanted to turn over some national parks to private business. But then the defeated bill was quietly secreted as an amendment in a giant budget bill that also included opening the Arctic National Wildlife Refuge to oil drilling.

Protecting the environment is one of those issues that legislators feel compelled to vote for in order to win reelection. On the other hand, big-business lobbies exert major pressure to kill many environmental bills. This Wicks cartoon pokes fun at the dilemma.

When Republicans won control of the Congress in 1994, the antienvironmental lobbies lost no time in seeking to slash the EPAs budget by a third, crippling its ability to enforce anti-pollution laws. The House voted for the bill that would do so in August 1995. The environmental lobbies aroused a storm of public criticism, which led the House to vote hastily to remove 17 of its EPA restrictions. But under pressure from business lobbyists, the House reversed itself and passed the original bill. President Clinton vowed to veto it if the Senate also passed it.[1]

In the next month lobbyists for Western special interests succeeded in getting the House to pass a huge antienvironmental bill. It reduced protection for endangered species; crippled federal conservation programs; slashed $6 billion from funds for the Interior Department; turned over public lands with valuable mineral deposits to mining companies for a fraction of their worth; opened Alaska's wildlife refuge to oil and gas drilling; wiped out major restrictions on logging in national forests; expanded grazing on public lands; allowed states and counties to push new roads through national parks, wildlife refuges, and wildernesses; turned over some 200 million acres (800,000 hectares) of national public lands to Western states; and permitted the use of offroad vehicles, powerboats, and skimobiles in wilderness areas. Under the bill the EPA would also be deprived of funds to regulate 17 different health problems, from oil refinery emissions to sewage runoffs into drinking water. As an extra concession to manufacturing lobbies, the bill even prohibited the Interior Department from issuing new standards requiring greater energy efficiency in refrigerators and air conditioners.

The Republican Congress also alarmed environmentalists by introducing lobbyist bills that would "weigh the cost" of environmental measures against human benefits. For example, if a regulation forbidding clearcutting a forest to protect an endangered species of bird or animal resulted in some lumber unemployment or profit loss, the bills would favor the lumber company's interests, not the wildlife's. In all the battles to abolish environmental laws, business lobbyists argued that the choice was between jobs and economic benefits on the one hand and protection for spotted owls and uninhabited wildernesses on the other.

Senator Orrin Hatch (R-UT) introduced a bill to permit the development of 6 million acres (2.4 million hectares) of wilderness in Utah, defending it as necessary for many rural counties in his state to survive economically. He also insisted that such development would not hurt the environment much. Advancing the interests of loggers and oil drillers in Alaska over protection of the environment, business lobbyists insisted they were simply trying to help the people of Alaska.

Vice President Al Gore, a conservationist, denounced Republicans on the Hill for a "jihad" (the Arab term for a holy war) against the environment that had allowed lobbyists from "the biggest polluters in America" to rewrite environmental laws.

In the Senate lobbyists sought a bill restricting federal powers to regulate public health, safety, and the environment. But public opposition was so strong that three efforts to pass it by Senate majority leader Bob Dole failed.

Efforts were also made by food-processor lobbyists to hamstring the Food and Drug Administration (FDA). These attempts did not sit well with the public in 1995, when 16 pesticides were found in 8 different baby foods.[2]

When the Republicans prepared a new bill making it easier for companies to challenge EPA regulations, House GOP leaders invited lobbyists into internal planning sessions. Judiciary Committee aides were dumbfounded when lobbyists for the utility industry were allowed to preside over a staff meeting on the bill. The lobbyists were even allowed to draft the legislation. Timber lobbyists also helped write the Senate version of revisions of the Endangered Species Act to open more natural habitats to lumbering.

Federal Election Commission records revealed that many election campaigns of Western legislators were heavily financed by lobbies for the oil and gas industries, mining and lobbying interests, developers, and growers.

Lobbyists for 14 energy companies won a 100-mile (160-kilometer) strip of Rocky Mountains land opened to mining, mainly through the aid of Senator Conrad Burns (R-MT). John Catchell, conservation director of the Montana Wilderness Association, observed, "His big campaign contributors got precisely the acreage they wanted."

Environmental lobbyists urged President Clinton to veto antienvironmental bills as a greedy power grab by business lobbies. A poll by conservative polltaker Frank Luntz showed that 62 percent of voters considered protecting the environment to be more important than easing regulations. Public opinion favoring those protections was shaped by the television, radio, and newspaper interviews with environmentalists from the Sierra Club, the Wilderness Society, and other naturalist lobbies.

"I foresaw a country with wetlands disappearing, air and water increasingly polluted, food and drugs unsafe," wrote columnist Anthony Lewis in *The New York Times*. "To my surprise, readers asked where I got such ideas. I got them from the precise terms of legislation ending in the House or already passed. . . . Industrial and other interests that give huge amounts of political money want to operate without worrying about the poisons they dump in the air or water or the destruction they do to our surroundings. Their lawyers and lobbyists actually wrote most of the 17 killer amendments."

Fighting back, President Clinton issued an executive order commanding companies doing business with the government to continue complying with federal laws requiring them to disclose their chemical emissions into the air. "There are people who want to strip away decades of public-health protection," he declared. "I intend to fight them every step of the way."[3]

Aware of growing public anger at attempts to scrap the EPA, moderate House Republicans joined Democrats in dropping the "17 killer amendments" to an EPA budget bill. The amendments were called a "back-door attack on environmental laws," inserted for the benefit of industry lobbyists. Those who sponsored them insisted that these amendments simply were intended to end "excessive EPA regulations" that hampered businesses.

They fought for and won reinstatement of the amendments. Their bill permitted industrial-waste runoffs to pollute lakes and streams, prevented higher standards for drinking water and clean air, and limited the requirement for public disclosure of toxic emissions from polluting factories.

The fight to permit water pollution also went on in state legislatures. In California, lobbyists for a bill to repeal a law requiring water agencies to meet safe drinking standards won passage from the state assembly. Mary Raftery, speaking for California environmentalist groups, declared: "Industry spent a lot of money to get a false message about this bill, and unfortunately it seemed to work on the Assembly floor." Democratic Assemblyman Byron Sher called the bill a "ploy by special interests who want to gut the California Safe Drinking Water Act."

The antienvironmental GOP bills in Congress hindered the cleanup of polluted U.S. rivers. In many states raw sewage and chemical wastes were discharged straight into rivers. The EPA found that in the New York metropolitan area alone, there were no fewer than 780 such discharge points, with the polluted waters flowing into the harbors of New York and New Jersey.

Industry lobbyists continued to persuade House Republican leaders to roll back what they called "unduly burdensome environmental regulations that weigh on local governments and restrain development."

On the other hand, in the clash between commercial interests and conservation, conservation often wins out. Conservationist lobbies wield a great deal of influence in state legislatures, and often effect passage of conservation laws.

U.S. News and World Report magazine reported on August 5, 1996, that the sport fishermen's main lobby, the 20,000-member Gulf Coast Conservation Association (GCCA), had spent millions of dollars on television commercials that helped win major legislation in Texas, Florida, Alabama, and Louisiana during the 1990s. The GCCA garnered public support by revealing that commercial fisheries were destroying wetlands and endangering many fish species.

LOBBYISTS WHO EXPLOIT THE LAND

Land lobbyists were active in 1848 when they persuaded Congressman Horace Greeley, chairman of the Public Lands Committee, to approve a bill selling government-owned alleged "swamp" lands bordering Lake Superior for bargain prices. Greeley failed to recognize the bill as a scheme by and for rich speculators.

"I, for one, was completely duped," he admitted later. "The consequence was a reckless and fraudulent transfer . . . of millions on millions of choice public lands which had not muck enough to accommodate a single frog."

In 1872 mining lobbies pushed a mining law through Congress that required the government to sell valuable federal lands to private companies for as little as $2.50 an acre. The law also permitted companies to search for minerals on federal lands by cutting roads through timber, as well as bulldozing and dredging or stripping land at will. Great cliffs of mine wastes blew into adjacent towns, polluting their air and streams.[4]

Efforts to cancel or reform the law were consistently beaten back by lobbyists for the Western mining industry. As recently as 1995 a furious Interior Secretary Bruce Babbitt was forced to approve the sale of 110 acres (45 hectares) of federal land in Idaho, which might contain minerals worth millions, to a private company for just $275. One year earlier a Canadian company paid $10,000 for land that had some $10 billion worth of taxpayer-owned gold deposits.[5]

The law also protected mining companies from having to pay any royalties to the government for valuable minerals found on these purchased federal lands.

Because of the powerful timber interests lobby, no legislation has been introduced to repeal or amend an 1864 land-grant law that enabled the big timber lobbies to gain control of about 40 million acres (16 million hectares) of Western forests. Their clients continued to overcut and export logs from these forests.

Dr. John Osborn, president of the Inland Empire Public Lands Council, calls the land-grant law the core of the current forest crisis. Congress has the power to repeal or amend that act, to allow the government either to regulate logging or to put the lands back into public ownership, but the rich timber lobby is unlikely to let that happen.

Clients of mining lobbies, who have won permission to operate in environmentally sensitive areas, have left behind 70 billion tons of poisonous tailings that contaminated the land and threatened the health of nearby homeowners. They have also left behind half a million dangerous open pits and mine shafts, and the pollution of some 12,000 miles (19,000 kilometers) of waterways.

"When the company gets the gold," declares Jim Barrett, chairman of the antimine Beartooth Alliance, "they'll be gone, but we will be here tomorrow. We will suffer forever."

THE AGRIBUSINESS LOBBY

The term "agribusiness" came into usage as corporations and wealthy investors gradually began buying up small farms and combining them in huge holdings. Agricultural lobbies were able to get Congress to pass large farm subsidies under the guise of helping the small family farms of America. In practice, by far the largest bulk of these subsidies went to agribusiness.[6] Many of the huge farm holdings were operated by absentee owners.

On the state level, agribusiness lobbyists were able to get bills favorable to them passed in rural America because state lawmakers indebted to them controlled redisricting—a method of rearranging voting districts so that elected rural representatives outnumbered those from the cities.

In the mid-1950s stacked grain bought from farmers and stored as reserves by the government, under pressure from the farm lobby, reached enormous quantities. The farm lobby then caused Public Law 480 to be passed, getting rid of the surplus by selling it cheaply or giving it away overseas, to make room for additional, but unnecessary, government purchases from agribusiness.

Food aid programs for poor people in the 1960s were shaped to suit the needs of agricultural interests, not those of the hungry. A 1966 Special Milk Program for poor children came about as a result of lobbying by the National Milk Producers Association. The National School Lunch Program was also originated by an agribusiness lobby as a new market for surplus crops.

The chairmen of agricultural committees in Congress now operate in the interests of agribusiness lobbies representing corporate farms, food industries, and growers associations. They not only control all food legislation, bottling up bills they oppose, but they also dominate the Department of Agriculture, whose budget is at their mercy. They have resisted all attempts to transfer food programs to the more impartial Department of Health, Education and Welfare (HEW).

In 1969 the agribusiness lobby won a $200 million farm program to help mostly big corporate farms increase their production. At the same time, ironically, the lobby also got the Agriculture Department to pay out $3.5 billion in subsidies to farmers to reduce surpluses by not overplanting their acreage. Most of these subsidies were paid to the top one third of farmers, approximately one million—which included all the wealthiest planters.

Many subsidies went to big landowners who lived away from their huge farms. For example, in Los Angeles, James G. Boswell received more than $4 million in federal subsidies to supplement his income from vast farm operations in California and Arizona.

"The farm programs," declared *New York Times* reporter William Robbins, "have been perpetrated by a group of men in Congress who exercise powers out of proportion to their numbers. Their sympathies have tended to go out to the larger landowners."

Large campaign contributions by agribusiness lobbies made certain that those legislators were constantly reelected.

In 1973, Senator Gaylord Nelson (D-WI) sponsored a bill to end handouts to the corporate farms. He charged the Agriculture Department with concealing from the public the extent to which big corporations had taken over agriculture and received the bulk of billions spent in farm aid programs. The agribusiness lobby saw to it that Nelson's bill was pigeonholed.

Farm lobbies don't particularly care whether they contribute campaign funds to Republicans or Democrats. Their interest is primarily in officials who occupy positions of power.

In 1994, Agriculture Secretary Mike Espy resigned after being criticized for taking favors from lobbyists for Tyson Foods,

Quaker Oats, and others. When the top lobbyist for Sun-Diamond Growers told a top agribusiness lobbyist, James Lake, that Espy had asked for $5,000 in illegal contributions to help pay off a brother's campaign debt, Lake arranged for the contributions and disguised them as personal donations. Lake pleaded guilty to charges of election fraud and had to resign from his lobbying firm.[7]

In 1995, lobbyists for the mining, grazing, logging, and chemical pesticide industries busily rewrote laws regulating those industries for the Republican Congress.

"The bill to relax rules for grazing on public land," observed *New York Times* columnist Anthony Lewis, "would benefit the computer billionaires William Hewlett and David Packard, who run cattle on nearly 100,000 acres (40,470 hectares) of federal land." Two thirds of the 170 million acres (70 million hectares) leased to ranchers is in unsatisfactory condition because of overgrazing.

The timber industry lobby saw to it that nearly $2 million was appropriated for new forest roads, so that the industry could transport its lumber. This lobby also sought to increase logging in Alaska's Tongass National Forest, the nation's largest temperate rain forest.

Newly elected Representative Sam Brownback (R-KS) had promised his Kansas constituents in 1994 that the Republicans would abolish wasteful programs like the one that paid McDonald's, Campbell Soup, Gallo Winery, and Sunkist Foods millions of dollars in taxpayer money to advertise overseas. But when he tried to eliminate the program, he found that lobbyists had stymied his attempt.

In California an agribusiness lobby assured passage of a bill allowing farmers to continue using a toxic pesticide on crops, despite the manufacturer's failure to provide health data. The pesticide had been found to cause dozens of serious injuries to

Showing the Department of the Interior as the champion of the various lobbies to exploit the Alaskan land, this cartoonist wryly captions this drawing, "Faster than a speeding developer, more powerful than a mining lobby . . ."

farm workers and to be harmful to the ozone layer. James Eller, a lobbyist for the California Farm Bureau, insisted, "There is no substitute for it. It is vital for some agricultural crops, especially strawberries."

6

Lobbying Efforts for Other Special Interests

PUBLIC UTILITIES

Early in the twentieth century the public utilities were charging customers exorbitant gas, electricity, and water rates. Congress, bought off by the utilities lobbies, refused to restrain them. When some governors set up regulatory commissions, the powerful utility lobbies saw to it that their state legislatures deprived the commissions of funds, and further hamstrung them by getting legislation passed that crippled their authority over rates and service.

But in 1935 a liberal New Deal Congress finally did pass a Public Utility Holding Company Act. This act broke up monopolies of public utility holding companies that controlled gas and electric companies. The Federal Power Commission was given authority to keep gas and electricity rates reasonable. The utility lobbyists thundered their outrage.

When the utility lobbies organized a telegram campaign to fight utility regulation, Senator Hugo Black introduced a bill to register and regulate all lobbies. Congress passed the bill, but then watered it down in committee to limit the lobby disclosures required. In 1938, Congress passed the Foreign Agents

Registration Act, requiring lobbyists for foreign countries or foreign companies to register.

At a House hearing by a Water and Power Subcommittee in 1995, Representative George Miller (D-CA) was outraged to see former Representative John Rhodes, a lobbyist for business and municipal water users, sitting with members of the committee. Miller objected, and Rhodes was forced to leave the dais. David Corn in *The Nation* called the cozy relations between the representatives elected in 1994 and utility lobbyists "brazen lobbying and conniving."

COMMUNICATIONS

In 1995 massive lobbying campaigns by the communications industry pressured the House to vote to relax restrictions against media monopolies. At the same time the House voted to deregulate phone companies and TV corporations.

"Consumers will wind up tipped upside down," warned Representative Ed Markey (D-MA), ranking Democrat on the House Telecommunications Subcommittee, "with money shaken out of their pockets to subsidize the deregulatory dreams of the largest monopolies in the country. The fiber-optic barons are in control."

Opponents charged that the bill would help business at the expense of consumers because real competition would take years to evolve, if it ever did. Insufficient safeguards let television cable and telephone rates increase and allowed a few big companies to dominate news, entertainment, and communications.

Nine consumer groups lobbied President Clinton to veto the bill. Vice President Al Gore called it "abhorrent to the public interest." But the bill was not surprising inasmuch as lobbyists for the communications and media industries contributed almost $38 million to congressional candidates between 1985 and 1994.[1]

THE MUNITIONS INDUSTRY[2]

The United Nations spends billions of dollars to deal with wars raging across the globe, pointed out Vesna Kesic, who heads the human rights group Be Active Be Emancipated. But the UN spends almost nothing to resolve international conflicts before they turn into war. "Could it be," Kesic asked, "that war is in someone's interest?"

When World War I broke out in Europe in 1914, munitions makers lobbied for a National Defense Bill to militarize America with huge armaments expenditures for "preparedness." The American Union Against Militarism, headed by the Reverend John Haynes Holmes, outraged the munitions lobby by demanding legislation that would outlaw munitions profits. In 1915, Representative Clyde H. Tavenner produced documents proving that the munitions industry had secretly conspired to stampede America into huge military appropriations leading to war. The real danger to America, Tavenner warned, did not come from overseas but from "a clique of men within this country who would tax the people until their backs break, simply that they might make profit supplying battleships, armor, and guns."

Similar concern was expressed in President Dwight Eisenhower's farewell address in 1961. He voiced his fear that the pressure of lobbies greedy for munitions contracts and fat profits, plus the power of the Pentagon, could stampede Congress into militarizing the nation dangerously. The climate for such pressure was provided by the Cold War—antagonistic relations with the Soviet Union—which many feared would explode into an actual war. Eisenhower was furious when he learned that defense industries had hired hundreds of retired Pentagon officers as lobbyists.

In February 1969, *The Nation* declared, "The services are under a cloud of suspicion that they were, and still are, in alliance with industrialists to spend billions on weapons that may satisfy the egos of high commanders but actually undermine national defense and make the whole world insecure."

In 1962, President John Kennedy's adviser on disarmament revealed that the munitions lobby had dangerously overloaded the United States with nuclear weapons. It was later learned that the lobby had done so by alarming Americans with vastly exaggerated figures about the number of such weapons in the Soviet Union.

"It is not inconceivable that we could blow ourselves up without help from the Russians," Kennedy's adviser warned him.

The effectiveness of military lobbies in Congress was highlighted in 1969 by *The Nation,* which revealed that Congress had voted only $5.9 million for the Arms Control and Disarmament Agency, but had paid $6.7 *billion*—one thousand times more—for the Pentagon's military research and development program.

In 1989, President George Bush sought to make former Senator John Tower (R-TX) secretary of defense. But at confirmation hearings by the Senate Armed Services Committee, Tower was rejected because of having served as a lobbyist for a half dozen defense contractors since he had left his seat in 1985. In two years he had received more than a million dollars from companies dealing with the Senate Armed Services Committee he had headed.

Munitions lobbyists press Congress for the biggest military contracts possible. In 1995 the Republican House obliged them by voting for $7 billion more in military spending than even the Pentagon had requested, including $1.4 billion for a ship the Navy did not want. Most of the excessive spending was for unnecessary military "pork" projects favoring certain legislators and their districts.

This pork was tucked away, largely invisible, in an $11 billion military construction budget. Some 80 percent went to munitions companies in the home states of members of the House National Security Committee.

In the House Appropriations Committee, Representative Martin Olav Sabo (D-MN) proposed a bill prohibiting defense contractors who received federal contracts and loans from using their own money for political campaign contributions. The committee's GOP members promptly voted it down.

The Senate responded to the munitions lobby by voting one military spending bill of over $242 billion, and another of more than $265 billion—$8 billion more than the Pentagon had requested. President Clinton threatened to veto all of Congress's pork-laden munitions bills.

In that same year lobbyists for Northrop Grumman Corporation, manufacturer of 20 existing B-2 Stealth bombers costing $2 billion apiece, were able to get a key House committee to vote another half billion dollars to keep B-2 suppliers in business. They did so over the protests of the Pentagon that the B-2s were actually unnecessary to national defense.

BANKS

The U.S. League of Savings Institutions, a powerful lobby, got Congress in 1980 to increase the level of savings and loan (S&L) insurance coverage to $100,000; to loosen accounting standards; to reduce reserves that the S&Ls were required to have on hand; and to permit bankrupt S&Ls to remain in business.

During the 1980s, significantly, the S&L lobby contributed more than $11 million to congressional candidates and political PACs. Some states, like California, let S&Ls invest 100 percent of their federally insured funds in speculative investments.

Charles Keating, head of the Lincoln S&L, whose lobby contributed heavily to the campaigns of five senators, was allowed to take risky gambles with the savings of investors and depositors. He also misappropriated bank funds. When his S&L went bankrupt, taxpayers had to pay $2.5 billion of government insurance in a bailout to depositors. Keating was sentenced to jail for theft.[3]

"The money lost by loose-cannon S&Ls didn't disappear," Amy Waldman observed in *The Washington Monthly*. "It . . . went into the pockets of politicians, as the thrifts spent vast amounts (of our money, it turns out) to keep government's hands off the industry. S&L interests invested more than $11 million in congressional candidates and party committees during the eighties. It was public campaign financing—in the service of a private interest."

The American Bankers Association (ABA) has more than 100 lobbyists, who have given almost $2 million to members of the House Banking Committee since 1991. In return their clients received "regulatory relief" and expanded powers to operate.

The bank lobby was upset when President Clinton proposed to have the government make student loans directly to the ABA. Alarmed at the loss of this business, the lobby pressured Congress into voting to scrap the president's program.[4]

When Representative Carroll Hubbard (D-KY) was defeated for renomination in 1992, he was hired as a lobbyist by the Independent Bankers Association of America. Interviewed by the Public Citizen lobby in 1993, Hubbard declared, "In law, it's not what you know, it's who you know." Subsequently he was indicted for several felonies, including conspiracy to impede the Federal Election Commission. He was sentenced to three years in prison.[5]

BIG BUSINESS

At the 1972 Democratic National Convention in Miami, former New York mayor Robert Wagner observed, "Rich men mostly want to rub shoulders with politicians. Give them the impression that they are close to the action, invite them to a meal at Gracie Mansion, and their campaign contribution will be in the next mail."[6]

Congress has been traditionally reluctant to curb corporations and industries that violate the public interest because these are also the major contributors to election campaigns through their lobbies. "The time is fast approaching," Representative Wright Patman (D-TX) said in 1974, "I am convinced, when Congress must decide just how far it is willing to go to allow these lobbyists to go on influencing legislation."

When Senator Russell Long (D-LA) chaired the Senate Finance Committee, he observed, "About 95 percent of campaign funds at the congressional level are derived from business." He pointed out that legislators helped their supporters get government contracts, voted to cripple government agencies that regulated industries, blocked agencies seeking to enforce environmental laws, and voted government subsidies for special interests.

Corporations whose lobbies seek changes in the law often want to rescind laws and regulations that protect the public in order to magnify corporate profits. Lobbyists' clients benefit financially when they don't have to obey restrictions against polluting drinking water with industrial wastes; against selling dangerous drugs or contaminated food; against selling unsafe products for children; or against poisoning the air with smoke-stack emissions.

Sometimes all it takes for a lobby to have its wishes prevail is a single legislator. This was the case in 1977 during the administration of President Jimmy Carter. The lobby for the AFL-CIO had won the support of Carter and the House for a bill that gave unions more power in collective bargaining.

But when the bill was introduced in the Senate, the U.S. Chamber of Commerce lobby got Senator Orrin Hatch (R-UT) to filibuster to delay legislation on the bill for five solid weeks, paralyzing all Senate action. Hatch held up legislation by reading the Bible and the phone book to an almost empty chamber. The Chamber of Commerce lobby, representing big business, also pressured other senators to refuse to vote to end Hatch's filibuster. Chagrined sponsors of the bill finally gave up and withdrew it.

In 1982, Ralph Nader's lobby, Congress Watch, pressured Congress to support the Federal Trade Commission's rule requiring used-car dealers to disclose serious defects in cars they sold. A used-car dealers' lobby hastily applied its own pressure, and Congress voted down the FTC regulation.

The American Truckers Association lobby paid legislators up to $2,000 each to make brief speeches at their breakfast meetings. It came as no surprise when those legislators voted against tax increases on motor fuel.

All through the 1980s the Department of Housing and Urban Development (HUD) gave lobbyists with Reagan administration connections project contracts for their clients. Former Secretary of the Interior James Watt denounced HUD's partisanship. But he also accepted $400,000 for using his political connections to get three HUD projects funded.

Congressional investigating committees revealed that these lobbyists had received $6 million in lobbying fees, which congressional Democrats denounced as "political payoffs."

State legislatures traditionally have been far more susceptible to big-business lobbies than to less affluent labor lobbies.

In California almost half a million workers earn the minimum wage or less. When legislative hearings on raising the minimum wage were held, lobbyists for businessmen claimed that any hike in that wage would increase prices to consumers and drive out many California businesses that could not afford higher wages.

The employers and manufacturers lobbyists also saw to it that Governor Pete Wilson called for a repeal of California's law requiring overtime pay for most people who worked more than eight hours a day. He claimed it was an economic drain on business. California Senate president Bill Lockyer, a Democrat, declared, "He may have some big contributors to his campaign funds who think it's a good idea."

When raising the minimum wage was brought up in Congress, business lobbyists saw to it that both houses of Congress bottled up the legislation in committees, claiming that it would hurt the economy and cost jobs. This was at a time when corporate profits were at a 25-year high, and after the nation's 500 largest companies had cut more than 3 million jobs in 10 years. Most gains in productivity went into higher profits, while workers' wages and fringe benefits were slashed by laying off employees and hiring lower-paid temporaries, with no benefits, in their place.

Eventually, however, Congress felt compelled to pass a bill raising the minimum wage a small amount over a period of time.[7]

Leaders of the auto, steel, and machinists unions, faced with declining memberships, business mergers that laid off workers, and a hostile political environment, decided to merge into a single organization of 2 million members, uniting their lobbying efforts in Congress to seek gains in labor legislation.[8]

In 1993 big-business lobbies pressured Congress into passing a North American Free Trade Agreement (NAFTA), allowing U.S. products into Mexico, and Mexican products into the United States, tariff free. The business lobbies insisted that increased sales to Mexico would create more jobs for Americans.

But Ralph Nader's Public Citizen lobby fought against NAFTA, warning that it would cause American firms to transfer their plants to Mexico to take advantage of cheap labor, while throwing more American workers out of jobs.

"NAFTA is causing the loss of existing jobs," Public Citizen charged in 1995, "while the new jobs that were promised aren't being created." It also pointed out that while American companies were enabled to cut their labor costs sharply, consumers in the United States were not given any benefit in lower prices for their products.[9]

Lobbyists for big business find open doors in Congress because their clients can afford large campaign contributions, representing a very small "investment" compared with the profits they stand to gain from legislation favoring their companies.

But lobbyists for the National Federaton of Independent Business Owners, representing more than 600,000 small businesses, also "spend millions because billions are at stake," said Charles Lewis, executive director of the Center for Public Indemnity in August 1994.

Late in 1995 the media began reporting that voters were beginning to feel apprehensive about the legislation that the new Congress was introducing, because it obviously favored business lobbies over the welfare of the public.

FOREIGN INTERESTS

When George Washington warned his fellow Americans to "beware of foreign entanglements," he could not have foreseen how one day foreign lobbies would have the power to pressure the American government for legislation and regulations favorable to their client nations.

In 1914 a lobby for U.S. investors in Haiti induced the Woodrow Wilson administration to send Marines to invade the island and protect their investments. The Marines stayed for twenty years, controlling Haiti until Franklin D. Roosevelt was elected to the White House and put an end to the American occupation. In 1930 dictator Rafael Trujillo of the Dominican Republic massacred 2,500 political enemies. In 1937 he massacred 12,000 "surplus" Haitians working on American-owned sugar plantations. He was denounced by a shocked American press.

A defector from his dictatorship revealed to *The New York Times* that a Trujillo lobby had spent $5 million on "some U.S. congressmen and State Department officials," and another $5 million on press agents to "take care" of the U.S. media. Trujillo also provided three-month vacations to U.S. government and business officials. The chairman of the Senate Agriculture Committee described Trujillo as "the sort of leader we need more of in Latin America." Trujillo's lobbyists won an increase in the Dominican sugar quota allowed into the United States.

After Chiang Kai-shek lost China to Mao Tse-tung's Red Army in 1948, he spent about $1.5 million of U.S. foreign-aid funds to hire American lobbyists to win support for denying recognition to Red China. His lobbyists, and subsequently those of the Taiwan government he founded, were successful in denying U.S. recognition to China for 31 years.

In 1961 a lobby by Cuban exiles in Miami induced the U.S. government to finance an invasion of U.S.-trained Cuban exiles to overthrow the Cuban regime of Fidel Castro. The result was a disastrous defeat of the invasion at the Bay of Pigs in Cuba, and a black eye for U.S. foreign policy.

Munitions lobbyists saw to it in 1964 that the Pentagon allocated a half million dollars for the sales promotion of U.S. arms to foreign countries. In 1966, *Newsweek* reported that Latin Americans were accusing the Pentagon of having supported military coups that had toppled nine civilian presidents in the previous four years.

President Jimmy Carter was embarrassed by his alcoholic brother Billy, who became a well-paid lobbyist for Libya, a nation the United States had denounced for sponsoring terrorism. He failed to register as a foreign agent as required by law,

Playing on the Boys Town slogan, "He's not heavy, He's my brother," cartoonist Pletcher shows President Jimmy Carter carrying the embarrassing burden of his brother's activity as a lobbyist for the nation of Libya.

and was also accused of improperly using his influence with the White House concerning military aircraft sales to Libya.

When Haitians sought to enter the United States illegally in small boats in 1991, the White House refused to grant them refugee status. Randall Robinson, a lobbyist, started a 25-day fast to try to reverse this policy. Haiti rewarded him by appointing his wife as its new Washington lobbyist for $12,500 a month.

During the 1980s some 100 foreign countries got around the law forbidding foreign campaign contributions in U.S. elections. They opened corporate subsidiaries in the United States and raised PAC campaign funds from their employees. Lobbyists for the Japanese-owned Sony Corporation of America, for example, donated $29,000 to California legislators, seeking repeal of a state tax affecting Sony products.[10]

While Richard Perle was assistant secretary of defense for international affairs, he was influential in securing $600 million a year in U.S. military assistance to Turkey. Leaving office in 1987, he organized a lobbying company a year later, which was paid $875,000 a year by Turkey to help the Turks receive more U.S. military and economic aid.[11]

The government of Taiwan, officially part of China, sought independent recognition from the United States. It spent more than $5 million in 18 months to employ as Washington lobbyists a former congressman, a former senator, a former Republican National Committee chairman, and many former congressional staffers as well as State Department and Treasury officials. The lobbyists gave out luxurious free trips to Taipei, the capital, to congressmen and government officials. They won permission for an official visit to the United States by Taiwan's president and access to important U.S. officials, infuriating the Chinese government.[12]

Michael Barnes, former chairman of the House Foreign Affairs Subcommittee on Latin Affairs, became a lobbyist for Haiti's president, Jean-Bertrand Aristide. Barnes, who had also headed President Clinton's election campaign in Maryland in 1992, lobbied the White House for support of Aristide. He won the sending of U.S. troops to Haiti to protect the Aristide regime at a cost to taxpayers of almost $1 billion.[13]

Because Libya had sponsored terrorist activities, Washington froze that country's assets in the United States. In 1992 two former Democratic congressmen, John Murphy, who had gone to jail for accepting a bribe, and David Bowan, were paid $675,000 by Libya to lobby for freeing those assets. They were fined $30,000 for failing to obtain a required Treasury Department license to operate as foreign lobbyists.

Castro-hating Cuban exiles in Miami succeeded in lobbying Washington to keep sanctions imposed against Cuba, and to deny U.S. recognition to its government. Their lobby pressured Congress to tighten the sanctions even further in 1995. American business executives seeking to do business in Cuba protested to the White House that the Cuban exile lobby was actually making U.S. foreign policy.[14]

Israel has a large lobbying organization in Washington, the American Israel Political Action Committee. The AIPAC has about 51,000 members, a $5 million annual budget, and some 83 employees in Washington and some states. Because most Americans sympathize with the little democracy surrounded by hostile Arab countries, the AIPAC lobby has been able to influence legislation strongly favorable to Israel.[15]

Japan was aware that American sentiment was hostile to it for closing many of its markets to U.S. goods while flooding the United States with Japanese products. Consequently Japan spent more than $100 million each year to hire hundreds of Washington lobbyists, many of them former high-ranking public officials with "connections" in Congress and the federal government. Its lobbyists spent another $300 million annually to influence American public opinion through the U.S. media.

Japanese economist Keitaro Hasegawa insisted that because Japan has such large investments in the United States, it "cannot stand by uninterested in changes of government in the United States." He defended the formation of PACs in Japan's U.S. subsidiaries to help elect Americans favorable to Japan's trade practices. Most legislators and government officials are reluctant to favor measures hurting Japan's business interests because they know that when they leave office many can get hired at $200,000 a year or more as lobbyists for Japan.[16]

A 1986 General Accounting Office (GAO) survey found that 76 former federal officials had become registered lobbyists for foreign nations—almost a third of them for Japan. Among them were 8 special assistants to the president, 5 assistants to the president, 4 retired generals, 15 congressmen, and 17 congressional staff members.[17]

THE MEDICAL INDUSTRY

Insurance and drug companies often hire former members of Congress and congressional aides to lobby for their interests in health-care legislation. A health-care lobby financed by the American Medical Association, the American Dental PAC, the American Nurses Association, and others spent more than $150 million to influence the outcome of health-care legislation. Four members of Congress each received more than $1 million in contributions.

Their contributions led to concessions made by Speaker Newt Gingrich to win the support of the AMA for the Republican Medicare and Medicaid bills. He agreed to relax federal regulations of doctors and their laboratories; to reduce taxes on private hospitals; to grant hundreds of millions of dollars in benefits for drug manufacturers; to withdraw cuts in Medicare fees to doctors; to allow doctors to refer patients to facilities in which they had financial interests; and to limit malpractice lawsuits.

A very poor and very sick citizen is being propped up by the doctors' lobby in an attempt to convince Congress that national health insurance is not necessary

"This is the biggest-scale lobbying effort that's ever been mounted on any single piece of legislation, both in terms of dollars spent and people engaged," declared Ellen Miller, executive director of the nonprofit Center for Responsive Politics. Most of those lobbying funds went to pay the lobbyists who buttonholed members of Congress on behalf of their clients. Some of the funds went directly into the campaign resources of legislators whose votes they hoped to get.[18]

The GOP presented their bill to slash $270 billion from Medicare as a plan to overhaul the program and save it from bankruptcy. The Democrats attacked it as an assault on senior citizens to finance a $245 billion tax cut for the wealthy. Speaker Gingrich invited 150 lobbyists to a meeting in the Capitol basement and reassured them they could continue to count on the tax cuts their clients demanded.

An Associated Press poll found that 56 percent of Americans over the age of 55 were worried about the GOP Medicare bill. Many who had voted for Republican congressmen in 1994 declared that they would not do so next time.[19]

On the other hand some medical lobbies have clearly promoted the public interest. According to an article by Dyan Machan in the August 12, 1996, issue of *Forbes,* a lobby by Children & Adults with Attention Deficit Disorder (CAWADD) was responsible for persuading Congress to pass the Disabilities Act of 1990. This new law provided special treatment and advantages for some 2.5 million children diagnosed as suffering from attention deficit disorder (ADD).

Such children are now treated with a daily dose of Ritalin. Not all parents agree with the treatment, but one New York mother boasted that her son's diagnosis and treatment had added 100 points to his combined verbal and math Scholastic Achievement Test (SAT) score.

Not surprisingly, the lobby for Ciba-Geigy, the manufacturer of Ritalin, had donated funds to CAWADD, a case in which a private manufacturer has helped to pass a law that presumably benefited 2.5 million children with ADD, as well as benefiting the company itself.

THE RELIGIOUS RIGHT

The Religious Right in America is a collection of conservative organizations—the Christian Coalition—that profess to speak for all Christians. Their lobbyists press chiefly for new legislation to outlaw abortion completely, to require prayer in schools, and to provide government vouchers for parents to send children to private or parochial schools. Their chief lobbyist is Ralph Reed.

Although outnumbered by opponents of their objectives, the Christian Coalition lobby is powerful because it is much better organized than its opponents. This lobby claimed the credit for getting out the vote that elected a Republican Congress in 1994. The Republican Party counts on its support in rounding up conservative votes in all state and national elections.

The Christian Coalition's political spokesman is Pat Buchanan, an unsuccessful candidate for the Republican presidential nomination in 1996. Buchanan threatened that if Republican moderates tried to drop or weaken the antiabortion plank from its platform at the Republican national convention, he might bolt the Republicans and start a third party. His position was endorsed by the Christian Coalition, whose lobby warned Republican lawmakers against defying it if they hoped to be reelected. The convention retained the plank.

The Christian Coalition lobby has also been the strongest voice for giving religion a place in our schools, from authorizing prayer in the schools to teaching religion. William J. Bennett, former secretary of education, urged lawmakers to pass a law permitting voluntary prayer in the schools. But the religious right was balked by other lobbies such as People for the American Way, which charged that allowing prayer in the schools, voluntary or not, would violate the First Amendment, which calls for separation of church and state.[20]

CONSUMERS AND PUBLIC INTEREST

In the 1970s consumers began to organize lobbies to protect their interests against Congresses dominated by big-business lobbies. Lobbies for consumer and environmental legislation included Consumer Union, minority groups, and senior-citizen organizations. They claimed that their lobbying was solely in the public interest.

Conservationist lobbies like the Sierra Club have prodded state and federal legislatures into passing laws curbing the destruction of our forests by lumber companies and the pollution of our lakes and rivers by industrial wastes.

The Consumers Union lobby has exposed the use of dangerous pesticides in agriculture and produce, resulting in the outlawing of the worst of such poisons. Consumer groups accuse even regulatory agencies set up to protect consumers, like the Food and Drug Administration (FDA) and the Federal Trade Commission (FTC), of protecting instead of regulating industries that violate consumer-protection laws. Some officials in these federal agencies are recruited from the very industries they are supposed to regulate and are often reemployed by those same industries to serve as lobbyists.

Two of the most effective consumer lobbies have been Common Cause, led by John Gardner, and Public Citizen/Congress Watch, led by Ralph Nader.

The "Nader's Raiders" lobby forced General Motors and others to recall defective cars and compelled many manufacturers

Ralph Nader has indeed been a busy bee for more than twenty years, flying from issue to issue as one of the few lobbyists working solely on behalf of the American people.

to curb deceptive sales practices and shoddy workmanship by exposing them. National advertisers were forced to cancel misleading ads. Farmers were forbidden to spray crops with the poisonous pesticide DDT. From 1965 through 1995 "Nader's Raiders" helped get at least 200 new federal and state laws passed on such issues as freedom of information and protection of the public's health, safety, and economic rights. Their exposes commanded much attention in the media.

While Nader and Gardner lobbyists succeeded in getting Congress to pass many consumer bills, these were often pigeonholed, delayed, or weakened by powerful committee chairmen who were supposed to reconcile House and Senate versions. And although federal regulatory commissions were supposed to protect the consumer, consumer lobbies often criticized them as more protective of negligent industries.

Common Cause declared that its objective was "returning the government to the people." Its lobbyists exposed big corporations with defense contracts that paid off helpful politicians with big campaign contributions. They also exposed how much money candidates were collecting and from whom. Some legislators were shown to have received donations from contributors who had business before committees on which those legislators sat or presided.

Business lobbyists pointed out angrily that the Common Cause lobby itself had spent over $442,000 in the 1982 off-year elections, almost 25 percent more than any other registered lobby.

"Many of the organizations that spend substantially more than we do don't report at all," Common Cause replied. Others, they added, used loopholes in the law requiring disclosures to conceal their real expenditures.

Legislators found that they couldn't ignore Common Cause. During the Watergate scandals, Common Cause filed lawsuits against President Richard Nixon's reelection committee, forcing the release of lists of illegal corporate campaign contributions of millions of dollars. This disclosure was a major factor in the fall of the Nixon presidency.

Other lobbies that work on behalf of the public interest include the Consumer Federation of America, People for the American Way, the Center for Responsive Politics, the Center for Public Integrity, the Wilderness Society, the League of Women Voters, Citizen Action, and Americans for Democratic Action, to name a few.

SENIOR CITIZENS

When senior citizens found themselves neglected by Congress, they organized the American Association of Retired People (AARP) to lobby for the interests of people over the age of 50. When the Republicans sought to reduce the national debt by slashing funds for Medicare and Medicaid, the health-care programs for the elderly and the poor, the AARP opposed it vigorously.

Senator Alan Simpson (R-WY) abruptly announced Senate hearings to question the AARP's tax-exempt status as a nonprofit organization. Intimidated, the AARP lobby dropped its opposition to the Republican program, and instead simply sought to negotiate compromises with Speaker Newt Gingrich and his staff. Gingrich observed dryly that the AARP had suddenly experienced "a change of heart."

TEACHERS

Another important nonbusiness lobby is that of the National Education Association (NEA) and the American Federation of Teachers (AFT). In 1982 the teachers' lobby contributed almost

The elderly were once a particularly vulnerable group when it came to influencing legislation, but their swelling ranks and the positive lobbying efforts of the American Association of Retired People (AARP) have changed that.

$1.5 million for 334 candidates in midterm elections, helping to elect 250. One of the lobby's rewards was the creation of a federal Department of Education.

In the 1994 congressional campaign teachers raised $3.5 million for Democratic candidates. The NEA alone outspent even the National Rifle Association, making it the fifth-largest PAC contributor in the nation.

"Teachers still have tremendous influence and power," observed Leo Troy, a labor expert at Rutgers University. Leaders of the NEA and AFT insist, however, that their goals are saving the public schools—for the good of the nation as well as for teachers. They deny that their lobbies are obstacles to school reforms demanded by many dissatisfied parents.

MOVIES AND TELEVISION

The movie and television industries have powerful lobbies working on their behalf. They were constantly put on the defensive by parents' groups, religious groups, and others complaining that too much sex and violence in movies and television programs were bad influences on children. An Associated Press Media general poll showed that 82 percent of Americans felt that movies contained too much violence; 80 percent that they contained too much profanity; 72 percent, too much nudity. A Gallup Poll in 1990 found that 77 percent wanted more careful regulation of sexual content.

L. Lowell Huesmann and Leonard Eron, University of Illinois psychologists, found that children who watched excessive amounts of television violence were more likely to commit violent crimes as adults. Using these studies as ammunition, the Christian right lobbied for censorship.

The movie industry, alarmed by this possibility, promised to reduce the shock factor in future films. The television industry also finally listed ratings similar to film ratings at the start of its programs to help parents avoid those deemed unsuitable for children.

In this way vigorous lobbying by citizens' groups can produce changes in objectionable industry practices, even though they do not succeed in winning new legislation.

7

American Cynicism and a Plan for Reform

"Huge numbers of people are alienated," observed Gordon Black, author of *The Politics of American Discontent,* "maybe as much as two thirds of the public. They're angry that government spending is out of control, that public policy is bought and sold by insiders, and nothing they can do will change it."

Poll after poll in 1995, by impartial as well as by Democratic and Republican pollsters, showed that most Americans had become deeply cynical about the U.S. political system. The surveys found that three out of four Americans distrusted their government. Four out of five believed that taxes were voted to help corporations more than people; that politicians did "whatever they want" once elected; and that the government was pretty much run by a few big interests looking out for themselves.[1]

Foreign observers agree that our system has serious flaws. "America has the most advanced influence-peddling industry in the world," observed the British *Economist.* "Washington's culture of influence-for-hire is uniquely open to all buyers, foreign and domestic. . . . Its lawful way of corrupting public policy remains unrivaled."

"There's no question the system is worse than ever," observed Ellen Miller, executive director of the nonpartisan Center for

Responsive Politics in 1995. "In the past we could always track special-interest favors; now it's happening so fast it's impossible to keep up."

Miller argued that piecemeal changes in lobbying laws would not correct congressional corruption. "The voters are going to demand much more radical change," she predicted.

In 1994 the Republicans had campaigned against Washington lobbyists as a blight on the political process. But after they had won Congress, they did not hesitate to put relentless pressure on lobbyists for donations to pay off campaign debts, and to build funds for reelection campaigns.

"These new Republican members," complained lobbyist Jack Abramoff, "are probably moving faster than [at] any time in history to exploit their power in fund-raising. It's more open and brazen than [at] any time before."

Sensitive to public criticism, the Senate in 1994 introduced a bill to tighten lobbying restrictions and ban their gifts. The Republicans filibustered the bill. When it failed to pass, lobbyists outside the Senate chamber applauded enthusiastically.

Representative George Miller (D-CA) introduced a bill called the Lobbyist Disclosure Act of 1995. It required lawmakers to reveal the source of any legislation, amendment, or congressional report, drafted by a lobbyist. In the Republican-controlled House, his bill went nowhere.[2]

In July 1995 public disgust with Congress led the Senate to pass hastily a new bill putting strict limits on gifts that senators could receive from lobbyists, including a ban on charity golf and ski outings, expensive meals, and tickets to sports and entertainment events, all paid for by special interests. The new Senate rules also put a $50 limit on lobbyist gifts, with an annual ceiling of $100 from any single source. Professional lobbyists were also required to register and disclose who their clients were, how much they were being paid, and the issues for which they were lobbying.

One loophole in the new Senate rules was that they required registration only of people describing themselves as "full-time" lobbyists. A large proportion of Washington lobbyists are lawyers, and few admit that they lobby full-time.

Senator Carl Levin (D-MI) told the Senate that its existing legislation was "a sham and a shamble." He added, "The people want us to change the way we do business in Washington."

Speaker Gingrich moved swiftly to pass his own reform bill through the House, hoping to silence growing public criticism. It banned House members from accepting free meals, sports or concert tickets, or other gifts from lobbyists; from receiving PAC gifts over $250; and from accepting free travel to participate in charity golf, tennis, or ski events. They were still free to accept expense-paid travel for themselves and their families to participate in business meetings.

On November 30, 1995, Congress, stung by polls showing that the public was appalled by the influence that lobbyists had over Washington, hastily passed a measure requiring lobbyists to disclose who their clients are, the issues they are lobbying, and the amount of money they are spending. Congress had passed such lobbying reform measures ten times before, yet all had eventually failed to emerge from the committees, to which House and Senate versions were sent to reconcile their differences.

President Bill Clinton called the new measure the first reform of the lobbying law in half a century. Promising to sign it into law, he declared it would "help restore the trust of the people in their government." He added, "This bill will change the way Washington does business. For too long, Washington's influence industry has operated out of the sunlight of public scrutiny. This new law will require professional lobbyists for the first time to fully disclose who they are working for and what legislation they are trying to pass or kill."

Representative John Bryant (D-TX), one of the bill's sponsors, said, "For untold numbers of years the American people have justifiably believed unseen forces were causing Congress to make decisions. Those forces will no longer be unseen, and this Congress is no longer going to be wined and dined."

Lawmakers hoped that the new legislation would soften public anger and disgust, fueled by TV news scenes of legislators frolicking with lobbyists on all-expense-paid trips to the Caribbean.

But Representative Porter Goss (R-FL), a backer of the new law, was nevertheless skeptical about how much would actually change. "Tradition dies slowly," he observed, adding, "those determined to skirt the new rules still will."

Wright Andrews, president of the American League of Lobbyists, noted that his colleagues were already looking for new ways around the new legislation. "Those with the biggest bucks will have even more disproportionate influence," he declared. "The reality is, any big interest is always going to have more influence than the citizen on the street because it has the interest, it has the money, it has the sophistication."

He predicted that powerful interests would pour even more money into grass-roots lobbying. And he noted that exemptions for gifts from "personal friends," and for "fact-finding" trips to sunny destinations, could still occur. Moreover, special interests could still continue to use their PACs to lobby legislators and call the expenses "campaign contributions" instead of lobbying expenses. The new law still did not reform campaign financing, despite the president's urging that it do so. So unlimited amounts of PAC and private money will continue to pour into and dominate election campaigns, with the largest spending a deciding factor in who gets elected.

Nor did Congress shut the "revolving door," which lets legislators and commissioners know they can count on employment later as well-paid lobbyists by the special interests whose bills they have favored. Nor did the new law prohibit the transfer of funds between candidates; nor prohibit fund-raising in nonelection years; nor forbid lobbyists to arrange for contributions.

One way to eliminate all the "pork" and lobbying favors written into legislation by Congress would be to empower the president with a line-item veto. This would allow the president to strike out such items from any bill before signing it into law.[3]

The Republicans demanded the line-item veto when Republican Presidents Ronald Reagan and George Bush were in the White House, with Congress held by the Democrats. But in 1995, with Democratic President Bill Clinton in the White House, and the Republicans controlling Congress, it was the Democrats who demanded the line-item veto to let Clinton "de-pork" congressional bills.

The budget bill passed by the House in 1995 had amendments for the benefit of lobbies for oil companies, ski resort operators, restaurants, coal companies, and other special interests. One provision benefited British Petroleum; another excused coal companies from providing health benefits for retired coal miners; marinas won a repeal of a tax on boat fuel; sheep farmers, funeral homes, and semiconductor companies won special benefits. The massive budget bill, said Representative Charles E. Schumer (D-NY), was "full of hidden goodies."

"We still don't know everything we voted on," complained Representative Anthony C. Beilenson (D-CA). Senator Bill Bradley (D-NJ) called the amendments "baubles and bangles" for special interests.

Ed Gillespie, spokesman for the House majority leader, defended the special-interest amendments as "serving the public interest" by protecting private property so that private industry could create more jobs.

THE TAXPAYER'S ROLE IN REFORM

Whether there is misgovernment by Washington or the states, it is too easy to blame political leaders for it. Those leaders did not get in power without the votes of the American people who supported them.

"The misgovernment of the American people," Lincoln Steffens once wrote, "is misgovernment *by* the American people." Legislators who misgovern us are *our* representatives. We often solve nothing by just "throwing the rascals out and electing a new bunch." The new bunch often proves just as bad, or worse. As voters, we need to insist upon political candidates of the highest integrity, instead of those with a record of representing the interests of rich and powerful lobbies.

"Maybe the taxpayers ought to hire lobbyists," wryly suggests Amy Waldman in *The Washington Monthly*. "At least then we would stand a chance."

Ralph Nader also wants people to have more of a public voice for their views. He proposes an Audience Network Coalition to enable citizens to produce their own radio and television programs, and command an hour on commercial stations daily. Nader also advocates more Citizens Utility Boards (CUBs) like those operating in four states. Funded by members' dues, these watchdog organizations intervene in rate cases and legislative hearings. The Illinois CUB alone, Nader points out, has saved ratepayers over $3 billion since 1983.

One basic reason that lobbying has become such a problem in American elections is that under the present system, running for public office is extremely expensive. The need for funds forces candidates to rely on lobbyists to supply them, obligating themselves to vote for bills desired by the lobbyists' clients.

"This is the No. 1 most important issue out there," declared Senator Bill Bradley (D-NJ). "You can't change anything until you deal with the money in politics."

This 1889 cartoon by Joseph Keppler was entitled "The Bosses of the Senate" for obvious reasons. The names are different—the Copper Trust, the Sugar Trust, the Paperbag Trust, the Standard Oil Trust, etc., as opposed to today's gun lobby, tobacco lobby, insurance lobby, industrial lobby, etc.—but the message is exactly the same as it was more than a century ago. Change the names on the bellies of the characters, update the dress a bit, and the cartoon could run on the op-ed page in tomorrow's newspaper.

The problem posed by PAC lobbies will never be solved until the amount of money that can be spent on election campaigns is strictly curbed by law. In most cases, big campaign contributions and special gifts to lawmakers often speak louder than words. Less electoral money would be needed if the period of campaigning is shortened. In Great Britain, for example, the campaign period for parliamentary seats is just two months.

We also need legislation curbing the use of campaign funds. When Representative Ronnie G. Filippo (D-AL) left Congress in 1990, he took with him almost a half million dollars in unused campaign funds. He set up a Washington lobbying firm, which promptly contributed $27,850 to congressional incumbents. Certainly it should be made illegal for legislators to use such funds for their private benefit.

If our election laws were changed to provide total public funding of qualifying candidates, private or PAC contributions could be banned, leveling the playing field for all candidates. Election laws could require television and radio to apportion free time for political speeches and debates.

Taxpayer payment for election campaigns would add some expense to the national budget. But this would be miniscule compared with the enormous savings for taxpayers by eliminating lobbyist cash and gift bribes to candidates, producing legislation that pours billions of dollars into the pockets of unscrupulous corporations and other special interests.

To stop the Washington "revolving door," we need a law that stretches to at least five years the time that must elapse before a former legislator or executive branch official can lobby Congress or government officials. Lobbyists who disguise their occupations as "strategic advisers" or "consultants" should be held strictly to laws that govern lobbying if they attempt to influence legislation or government regulations.

It certainly should be illegal for any lobbyist to write any legislative bills or government regulations. In November 1993, for example, former legislative aide Jan Schoonmaker turned lobbyist was allowed by a House committee to help write a bill that would compel the Pentagon to finance university science projects. Lobbyists are not elected officials and have no right to write the laws.

The principal forces on the front lines fighting political corruption are the organizations that lobby in the public interest, like Common Cause, Citizen Action, and the Center for Responsive Politics. They attempt to bring public pressure on lawmakers to oppose bills representing corporate greed, and they try to convince lawmakers that they will gain more supporters by voting for bills in the public interest, and against those that are not.

These organizations deserve public support. Common Cause has proposed legislation for campaign reform. It would reduce dramatically the role of PACs and other special-interest money in congressional elections; place limits on all campaign spending and the use of personal wealth in campaign funds; prohibit the contribution of millions of dollars to political parties and campaign committees; ban lobbyist gifts to legislators and government officials, and their staffs; ban the transfer of campaign cash between candidates; prohibit off-year fund-raising; and prohibit lobbyists from arranging for campaign contributions to candidates whom they lobby.

The urgent need for genuine reform of the lobbying laws was demonstrated dramatically once again in the 1996 election campaign. Common Cause charged both the Democratic and Republican parties with blatantly breaking the law. Both parties evaded the law limiting campaign contributions to each candidate by using the scheme of "soft money." The law permitted corporations to give donations of any size—"soft money"—to political *parties,* rather than candidates. The parties then distributed the dollars to their candidates.

Republicans raised $76 million in soft money from January 1995 to June 1996, from such big corporations whose interests they favored as Archer Daniels Midland, Gallo Wine, and the tobacco companies. The Democrats solicited $425,000 from an Indonesian businessman whose family controlled the Lippo Group, after the vice chairman of Lippo's California banking subsidiary, John Huang, was given a top Commerce Department job by the Clinton administration in 1994. In this position Huang was able to influence American foreign policy and business relations with Indonesia.

The nation was once more appalled by the lobbying scandal involving both political parties.

It may take a new generation of Americans to force action that will truly reform our electoral system.

NOTES

CHAPTER ONE

1. The Associated Press, July 25, 1995.
2. Jeffrey H. Birnbaum, *The Lobbyists* (New York: Random House, 1971), p. 7.
3. Ernest and Elizabeth Wittenberg, *How to Win in Washington* (Cambridge, Mass.: Basil Blackwell, 1989), pp. 49–52.
4. Vincent Buranella, "James Madison," The American Heritage Pictorial History of Presidents of the United States, pp. 129–130.
5. Birnbaum, p. 9.
6. Jules Archer, *The Extremists* (New York: Hawthorn Books, Inc., Publishers, 1969), p. 124.
7. Bill Adler, "Presidential Wit," Truman press conference, December 2, 1948 (New York: Trident Press, 1966), p. 177.

CHAPTER TWO

1. "Congress Members Visiting Warm Places," The Associated Press, February 16, 1996.
2. "Lawmakers Live Well for Free," The Associated Press, March 12, 1996.
3. Jeffrey H. Birnbaum, *The Lobbyists* (New York: Random House, 1971), pp. 234–360.
4. "Pork Projects Funded Despite Budget Bluster," *The New York Times,* July 30, 1995. Also: "Clinton Wields Threat of Veto," The Associated Press, August 3, 1995.
5. Michael Pertschuk, *Giant Killers* (New York: W. W. Norton, 1986), p. xx.
6. John W. Wright, editor, *The Universal Almanac, 1991* (Kansas City/New York: Andrews and McMeel, 1990), p. 84.
7. Common Cause mailing.
8. Richard L. Berke, "Congress's New GOP Majority Makes Lobbyists' Life Difficult," *The New York Times,* March 25, 1995.

9. Eric Pooley, "Attack of the Killer D'Amato," *Time,* September 11, 1995.
10. Jeffrey H. Birnbaum, "The Thursday Regulars," *Time,* March 25, 1995.
11. "G.O.P May Accelerate Anti-Lobby Debate," *The New York Times,* September 18, 1995.
12. Viveca Novak, "The Trouble with Newt," *Time,* October 16,1995. Also: "House Ethics Panel Questions Gingrich," The Associated Press, July 28, 1995.
13. *Time,* November 15, 1993, p. 28.
14. Fred Barnes, "When Congressmen Turn Lobbyists," *The Readers Digest,* March 1995, p. 90.
15. Mchael Lewis, "The Access Capitalists," *The New Republic,* October 18, 1993.
16. Barnes, "When Congressmen Turn Lobbyists," p. 91.
17. "A New Maxim for Lobbyists," *The New York Times,* November 3, 1993.

CHAPTER THREE

1. Leonard Lurie, *Party Politics: Why We Have Poor Presidents* (New York: Stein and Day, 1980), pp. 108–109.
2. Jack Anderson with James Boyd, *Confessions of a Muck-raker* (New York: Random House, 1979), pp. 222–226.
3. Ibid., pp. 275–276, 279–287, 301–309.
4. Ibid., p. 329.
5. John Leo, "Cash the Check, Bob," *U.S. News & World Report,* September 18, 1995.
6. Michael Isikoff, "With Friends Like Hillary," *Newsweek,* August 14, 1995.
7. "Another Queasy Experience," *Newsweek,* September 15, 1995.

CHAPTER FOUR

1. Leonard Lurie, *Party Politics: Why We Have Poor Presidents* (New York: Stein and Day, 1980), pp. 178–179.
2. "Clinton Gets Back to Work," *Newsweek,* September 11, 1995.
3. Personal interview with George Seldes, May 8, 1991.
4. "A Whiff of Smoking Guns," *Newsweek,* August 7, 1995.
5. The Associated Press, July 26 and 31, August 14 and 24, 1995. Also: *Santa Cruz Sentinel,* August 2, 1995.
6. "Firing Up the Politics of Teen Smoking," *Newsweek,* August 21, 1995. Also: "Clinton Takes on the Tobacco Industry," *U.S. News & World Report,* August 21, 1995.

7. Philip Morris ad in *Time,* September 11, 1995.
8. *Time,* June 16, 1995.
9. "Women Plead for Peace," The Associated Press, August 3, 1995. Also: "NRA Criticized for Aggressive Tactics," *The New York Times,* July 30, 1995, and Gloria Borger, "Capitol Hill's Two-Ring Circus," *US. News & World Report,* July 31, 1995.
10. "Taking Aim: NRA/Clinton Duel," *The Boston Globe,* October 15, 1995.
11. *Santa Cruz Sentinel,* September 5, 1995.

CHAPTER FIVE

1. John Cushman, Jr., "House Reverses Vote on EPA Enforcement," *The New York Times,* August 1, 1995. Also: Bob Cohn and Daniel Glick, "It's Not Just Owls Anymore," *Newsweek,* November 4, 1995.
2. "Pesticides Found in Baby Foods," The Associated Press, July 26, 1995. Also: "This Land Is Whose Land?" *Time,* October 23, 1995.
3. *Newsweek,* September 4, 1995. Also: *The Nation,* May 1, 1995.
4. "Clinton Issues Policy Directive," *The New York Times,* August 9, 1955. Also: John Greenwald, "Arsenic and Old Mines," *Time,* September 25, 1995.
5. "Potentially Rich Acres of Idaho Land Sell for $275," The Associated Press, September 7, 1995.
6. Fred Barnes, "When Congressmen Turn Lobbyists," *The Reader's Digest,* March 1995, p. 91. Also: "The GOP Needs Some Education," *U.S. News & World Report,* September 11, 1995, p. 74; "Assembly Okays Exemption on Methy Bromide Requirement," McClachy News Service, September 7, 1995; Robert J. Samuelson, "The Price of Politics," *Newsweek,* August 25, 1995, p. 65; Thomas Rosenstiel, "Pork Goes Republican," *Newsweek,* August 14, 1995, p. 34; and "Reaping a Bitter Harvest," *U.S. News & World Report,* July 24, 1995, p. 39.
7. "Lake Pleads Guilty; Espy Faces Scrutiny," The Associated Press, October 26, 1995.

CHAPTER SIX

1. Daniel Pearl, "Telecom Bill Will Usher in New Cable Era," *The Wall Street Journal,* August 4, 1995. Also: Jeanne Aversa, "House Passes Bill Reforming Telecommunication," The Associated Press, August 5, 1995; "Consumer Groups Rally for Telecom Bill Veto," Hearst Newspapers, August 5, 1995; "Regulations Ease Rate Controls on AT&T," The Associated Press, October 13, 1995.

2. "Women Plead for Peace," *Santa Cruz Sentinel*, September 2, 1995. Also: Personal interview with George Seldes (May 8, 1991); Ernest and Elisabeth Wittenberg, *How to Win in Washington*, pp. 57–59; Jeffrey H. Birnbaum, *The Lobbyists*, pp. 55–58; "Budget Impasse Forecast," The Associated Press, July 29, 1995; Bruce B. Auster, "Help Yourself to Some Pork," *U.S. News & World Report*, July 24, 1995; "Senate Votes $242 Billion for Military," *The New York Times*, September 7, 1995; "A Stealthy Disclaim," *U.S. News & World Report*, July 24, 1995; and Mortimer B. Zuckerman, "The GOP Needs Some Education," *U.S. News & World Report*, September 11, 1995.

3. Amy Waldman, "Move Over, Charles Keating," *The Washington Monthly*, May 1995, pp. 26–32.

4. "President Blasts Banks for Ditching College Loans," The Associated Press, September 12, 1995.

5. Fred Barnes, "When Congressmen Turn Lobbyists," *The Reader's Digest*, March 1995, p. 91.

6. Leonard Lurie, *Party Politics: Why We Have Poor Presidents* (New York: Stein and Day, 1980), p. 120.

7. "Senate Rejects Wage Vote," The Associated Press, August 2, 1995.

8. Kevin Galvin, "Large Unions Planning Merger," The Associated Press, undated.

9. Marc Levinson, "Oh No, Not NAFTA Again!" *Newsweek*, September 25, 1995.

10. Pat Choate, *Agents of Influence* (New York: Alfred A. Knopf, 1990), p. 109.

11. Ibid., pp. 51–52.

12. "Taiwan's Clout," *U.S. News & World Report*, July 24, 1995.

13. Barnes, "When Congressmen Turn Lobbyists," pp. 92–93.

14. "Economic Pressure Can Help Heal Rift with Cuba," *The New York Times*, September 9, 1993.

15. Ernest and Elizabeth Wittenberg, *How to Win in Washington* (Cambridge, Mass.: Basil Blackwell, 1989), pp. 86, 91–92.

16. Choate, *Agents of Influence*, pp. x-1, 34, 121, 175.

17. Ibid., p. 19.

18. *Time*, September 4, 1995, pp. 24–29 and October 20,1995, pp. 25, 40. Also: "GOP Bends to Industry Lobbyists," *The New York Times*, October 15, 1995.

19. "GOP Plan Riles Seniors," The Associated Press, November 3, 1996.

20. "CBS Reports: Faith and Politics, Too: The Christian Right," Broadcast, September 7, 1995. Also: Scott Williams, "CBS Explores the Christian Right," The Associated Press, September 7, 1996, and "Christian

Coalition Seeks 100 Percent GOP Control," The Associated Press, September 10, 1995.

CHAPTER SEVEN

1. Laura Myers, "Pollsters: Cynicism Grips the Electorate," The Associated Press, August 2, 1995. Also: Daniel Corn in *The Nation,* May 1, 1995.
2. Adam Clymer, "Senate Backs New Lobbyist Rules," *The New York Times,* July 25, 1995.
3. "Clinton Vetoes Budget Bill," The Associated Press, October 4, 1995.

BIBLIOGRAPHY

Andersen, Jack, with James Boyd. *Confessions of a Muckraker.* New York: Random House, 1979.

Archer, Jules. *Washington vs. Main Street: The Struggle Between Federal and Local Power.* New York: Thomas Y. Crowell, 1975.

_____. *Winners and Losers: How Elections Work in America.* San Diego: Harcourt Brace Jovanovich, 1984.

_____. *The Extremists: Gadflies of American Society.* New York: Hawthorn Books, 1969.

_____. *Hunger on Planet Earth.* New York: Thomas Y. Crowell, 1977.

_____. *Hawks, Doves and the Eagle: America's Struggle For and Against War.* New York: Hawthorn Books, 1970.

_____. *Angry Abolitionist: William Lloyd Garrison.* New York: Julian Messner, 1969.

_____. *Fighting Journalist: Horace Greeley.* New York: Julian Messner, 1966.

Berman, Harold J., ed. *Talks on American Law.* New York: Vintage Books, 1961.

Birnbaum, Jeffrey H. *The Lobbyists.* New York: Times Books, 1992.

Burns, John. *The Sometime Governments.* New York: Bantam Books, 1971.

Caro, Robert A. *The Path to Power.* New York: Vintage Books, 1981.

Cater, Douglass. *Power in Washington.* New York: Vintage Books, 1964.

Choate, Pat. *Agents of Influence.* New York: Alfred A. Knopf, 1990.

Cigler, Allen J., and Burdett A. Loomis, eds. *Interest Group Politics, Washington, D.C.:* Congressional Quarterly Press, 1986.

Common Cause. *How Money Talks in Congress*. Washington, D.C.: Common Cause, 1973.

Deakin, James. *The Lobbyists*. Washington, D.C.: Public Affairs Press, 1966.

Drew, Elizabeth. *Politics and Money: The New Road to Corruption*. New York: Macmillan, 1983.

Ehrenhalt, Alan. *The United States of Ambition: Politics, Power and the Pursuit of Office*. New York: Times Books, 1991.

Green, Mark J., James Fallows, and David R. Zwick. *Who Runs Congress?* New York: Bantam Books, 1972.

Grieder, William. *Who Will Tell the People?* New York: Simon & Schuster, 1992.

Jackson, Brooks. *Honest Graft: Big Money and the American Political Process*. New York: Alfred A. Knopf, 1988.

Lurie, Leonard. *Party Politics*. New York: Stein and Day, 1980.

McCullough, David. *Truman*. New York: Simon and Schuster, 1992.

Moscow, Warren. *What Have You Done for Me Lately?* Englewood Cliffs, N.J.: Prentice Hall, 1967.

Nader, Ralph, and William Taylor. *The Big Boys: Power and Position in American Business*. New York: Pantheon Books, 1986.

Pearson, Drew, and Jack Anderson. *The Case Against Congress*. New York: Simon and Schuster, 1968.

Pertschuk, Michael. *Giant Killers*. New York: W. W. Norton, 1986.

Schriftgiesser, Karl. *The Lobbyists: The Art and Business of Influencing Lawmakers*. Boston: Little, Brown, 1951.

Secretary of State, California. *Report—Lobbying Expenditures and the Top 100 Lobbying Firms for 1993, 1994*.

Seldes, George. *Facts and Fascism*. New York: In Fact, Inc., 1943.

Smith, Judity G. *Political Brokers: Money, Organization, Power and People*. New York: Liveright, 1972.

Steffens, Lincoln. *The Shame of the Cities*. New York: Hill and Wang, 1957.

Stern, Philip M. *The Best Congress Money Can Buy*. New York: Pantheon Books, 1986.

Thayer, George. *The Farther Shores of Politics.* New York: Simon and Schuster, 1967.

Winter-Berger, Robert N. *The Washington Pay-Off.* New York: Dell, 1972.

Wittenberg, Ernest and Elisabeth. *How to Win in Washington.* Cambridge, Mass.: Basil Blackwell, 1989.

Ziegler, Edward. *The Vested Interests.* New York: Macmillan, 1964.

INDEX